Baby & Child Care

Solutions by a Specialist

Baby & Child Care

Solutions by a Specialist

Dr. Sivaranjani Santosh
MD Paediatrics (JIPMER)

UNICORN BOOKS

Publishers
UNICORN BOOKS
F-2/16, Ansari Road, Daryaganj, New Delhi-110002
☎ Ph.: 011-23262683, 23250704, 45644782
E-mail: info@unicornbooks.in • *Website:* www.unicornbooks.in

ISBN 978-81-7806-218-1

New Reprint Edition: 2026

Printed at Manipal Technologies Limited, Manipal

Dedicated to the ever loving memory of my mother late Mrs. Lakshmi Devi who had always been and who will continue to be my inspiration in all my endeavours

Contents

SECTION II : Six Months to Six Years

Foreword

We live in a world of plummeting medical standards. Everywhere one looks, there are signs of ignorance and indifference. When parents are confused about child care, the world carries on around them blind to their plight. Dr. Sivaranjani Santosh, a paediatrician by training from JIPMER, an Institution of National importance, out of a profound stirring has eased the way for an objective perception on child care through this book. It has been offered in a spirit of helpfulness and it would indeed prevent misconceptions, denials amongst mothers and their families.

It is no wonder new parents have many questions as normal babies vary so much in growth and behaviour. Controversies surround the need for expensive treatment options mystified by the medical world and statements in the lay press on unsubstantiated data compound the picture.

Information is power and the author has empowered the reader with up to date information, reflecting the current ethos of child care. Every section of the book deserves praise as they are comprehensive without overwhelming details. Physiology of pregnancy, child care, F A Qs on vaccination, common childhood illnesses, resuscitation measures, and the part on adopting a child are all well written The simple and clear expressions of Dr. Sivaranjani Santosh reflect her communication skills.

The plethora of information, photos which enliven the pages of the book both hold the reader's attention and help to guide one to the basics of maternal and child care. The text is practical and the reader will find enjoyment and instruction in this book. The author and her team richly deserve our congratulations for their meticulous and painstaking efforts.

Professor (Dr) S. Mahadevan

JIPMER, Puducherry

4th November 2009

❑❑❑

Preface

This book, *'Baby & Child Care: Solutions by a Specialist'* was basically conceived when my friends started consulting me over phone about common day-to-day problems regarding their babies. Having a newborn raises a myriad of questions in the mother's mind and understandably so! This book was originally written keeping newborns and infants in mind. It was only on further discussion with friends and Dr. Ashok Gupta, MD, Pustak Mahal that the sections on pregnancy care, care of toddlers and young children and related laws were added.

This book covers about the normal development of a child, day-to-day care, health issues, behavioural issues and emergencies related to infants, toddlers and young children. This book is well equipped with pictures and illustrations to help mothers understand the normal development of a child, common problems and common procedures related to the baby. I believe that mothers will benefit immensely from these illustrations and photographs. The common day-to-day queries of mothers have been answered in a 'question and answer' format to make it more interesting for mothers to go through the book. It is almost like I am discussing the concerned issue across the table with the mother. I have taken pains to keep the answers as concise and crisp as possible; at the same time conveying all the relevant information to the mother.

It is very important to realize that this book should not be used to diagnose and treat illness in children, but should just serve as a guide in dealing with common problems and to realize when it is time to consult your doctor.

The section on behavioural problems has been added to guide mothers to tackle these problems sensitively and sensibly. The section on emergencies should be read beforehand, as there may be no time to refer to the book in times of emergency.

I hope this book will be of good help to mothers in taking care of themselves and their children in the best possible way.

Dr. Sivaranjani Santosh

❑❑❑

Acknowledgements

I am deeply indebted to Dr. N. Chandra kumar, senior resident, neonatology, AIIMS, New Delhi for his contribution towards photos, critical review of the manuscript and relentless support during the process of writing this book. Without his contribution, this book would be incomplete.

I am thankful to Dr. V.P. Jyotsna, Consultant Obstetrician and Gynaecologist, Yashoda Hospitals, Hyderabad for her contribution towards the section on 'Pregnancy Care'.

I express my gratitude to my uncle, Mr. M. V. Durga Prasad, Advocate, High Court, Hyderabad for his encouragement, guidance, review of manuscript and his contribution towards the section on 'Related Laws'.

I am thankful to Dr Jhuma Sankar, Assistant Professor, Paediatrics, Ram Manohar Lohia Hospital, New Delhi for her contribution to the photos and review of the manuscript.

I am thankful to Dr Aparna Mahendru, HOD, Biochemistry, National Dental College, Derabassi, Punjab for review of manuscript and help in supplying materials for photography.

I am thankful to the editorial team of 'Unicorn Books' for their encouragement and valuable suggestions.

I would never have been able to complete this book if it were not for my husband, Dr. R. Santosh, Department of Endocrinology, PGIMER, Chandigarh. His encouragement, review of manuscript, formatting and editing of the manuscript, and photography played a very crucial role in giving final shape to this book.

This book would be lifeless and barren if it were not for my daughter, Aditi Santosh. She has cooperated perfectly for the photos. Above all, she has given me the first-hand experience at bringing up a child and thus taught me the art of bringing up a child in the best possible way.

Last but not the least, I am thankful to my father, Dr. M. Rama Prasad, for his timely advice and support, other family members who have encouraged me throughout the project, my teachers who have taught me Paediatrics and all the children and their mothers for helping me become a good paediatrician and also for helping me with the photographs for this book.

❏❏❏

Introduction

Child care starts even before you conceive. First and foremost, you have to be ready both physically and mentally to go through your pregnancy. Child care is going to be very stressful; mostly because of the lack of sleep in the earlier part and the demands that the child places on your time and energy in the later part. Nevertheless, if you try to enjoy being a mother and avoid thinking about the unavoidable stress, then motherhood can be more enjoyable than scary.

I would like to give a brief idea about how pregnancy occurs. All females have 2 ovaries in their pelvis. Ovaries are the place where ova (eggs) are produced. At puberty a lot of hormonal changes take place in a girl's body; and the ovaries start releasing an ovum (egg) every month. This egg travels via a tube (fallopian tube) to reach the womb. Fertilization occurs when the sperm manages to penetrate the egg while in the fallopian tube. These sperms are deposited in the vagina of a female by a male during the process of sexual intercourse. They travel up and reach the fallopian tube via the womb. One of them may manage to fertilize the egg. If fertilization doesn't occur, the egg and the tissues lining the womb are shed. This is called menstruation (periods, menses). If fertilization occurs, pregnancy will result. The fertilized egg will reach the womb and establish itself there. A lot of hormones are produced and lots of tissues build up in the womb to sustain the new life. After about 9 to 9 ½ months, the baby will be delivered.

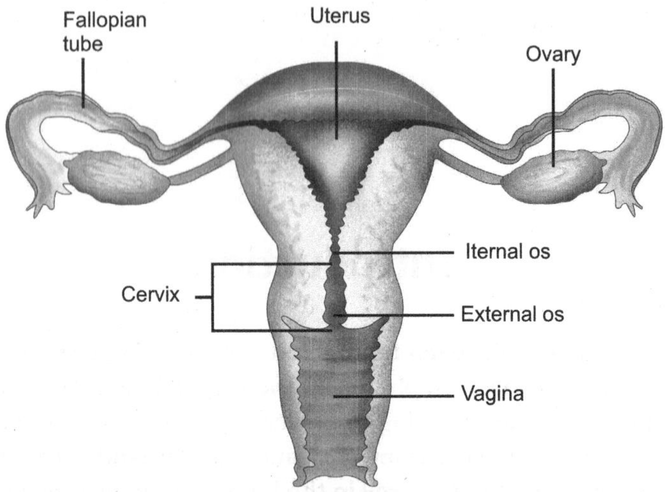

Fig: I Female genital tract

Your ? s My Answers:

What is the right time for sexual intercourse if a couple is planning for pregnancy?

14 days before the next expected menstrual period is the time when egg is released by the ovary (i.e. menstruation occurs 14 days after the release of the egg). So women with regular cycles can easily calculate the date. For example, if a lady gets her periods every 30 days and is expecting her next period on 15th November, then she will ovulate (release egg) on 1st November. Intercourse around this time is ideal for those couples planning for pregnancy..

It is difficult to predict the time of release of the egg if the periods are irregular. Vaginal secretions increase during the time of release of the egg, and body temperature rises. These changes can give the woman an idea that she has ovulated, especially if she is having irregular cycles and is not able to calculate the time of release of the egg. It is better to discuss this aspect with the obstetrician in case of any doubt.

What determines the sex of the baby?

Women have a pair of sex chromosomes in all their cells. They are named 'X'. Men have one 'X' chromosome and one 'Y' chromosome. Eggs from the female carry one of the 'X' chromosomes. Sperms carry either one 'X' chromosome or a 'Y' chromosome. When a sperm carrying 'X chromosome meets up with the egg (which always carries only 'X' chromosome) an 'XX' pair forms and the baby will be a girl. If the sperm carrying 'Y' chromosome meets up with the egg a 'XY' pair forms and the baby will be a boy. So sperm, and thus the man is responsible for determining the sex of the baby.

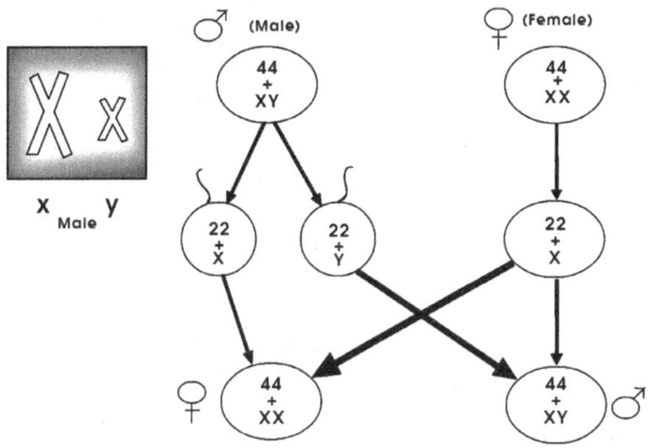

Fig: 2 Illustration to explain about what determines the sex of the baby

How does my baby grow in the womb?

The cell formed by the union of egg and sperm is called zygote. This single cell travels from the fallopian tube to the womb and gets attached to the lining of the womb. This zygote will multiply, mature and differentiate into various organs of the baby. Baby develops connection with the mother's womb initially through small blood vessels penetrating the lining of the womb. These vessels, the surrounding membranes and tissues form the placenta. Later on; the placenta enlarges and is connected to the developing baby by means of the umbilical cord. Baby gets all the nutrition and oxygen from the placenta, and sends its waste products to the placenta via this umbilical cord. When the baby is delivered, this umbilical cord is cut and clamped around 2 inches from the baby's end. The placenta along with its share of the umbilical cord gets expelled from the womb. The baby's umbilical cord dries up, gets shed few days later, and leaves behind the umbilicus or belly button on the baby.

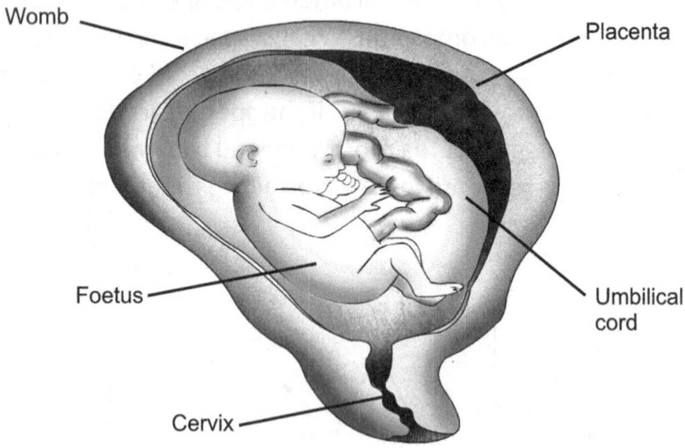

Fig: 3 Placenta and umbilical cord

I am planning to go in for my first baby. How do I ensure that my baby grows well?

There are many things that you have to take care of before and after you conceive.. Before explaining about those things, I would like to tell some basic facts about how a baby develops inside the womb. Baby starts out as a single cell and then grows up into the beautiful baby that you are looking forward to. Most of the baby's systems; i.e. heart, brain, spinal cord and nerves, eyes, ears, nose, mouth, limbs, genitals etc are formed within the first few weeks of conception i.e. around 10 weeks from your last menstrual period. Any insult to the developing baby at this stage will result in major defects.

Follow the following tips to ensure healthy growth of the baby

- Deficiency of Folic acid, especially in the first 10 weeks of pregnancy, will result in defective formation of the baby's brain and spinal cord. Therefore, it is necessary for the mother to eat lots of green leafy vegetables even before conception. Consult your obstetrician and start folate supplementation also before conception. Folate is prescribed to the pregnant woman for the very same reason. So, do take folate everyday as prescribed by your obstetrician.

- Ensure that you have a normal haemoglobin level even before conception. Measuring haemoglobin level in your blood is to rule out anaemia (thinness of your blood). Iron is very important for the formation of haemoglobin. You will have to provide enough iron for the formation of your baby's blood in addition to your own. You can talk to your obstetrician about this and take iron capsules if necessary. Iron supplementation is needed during pregnancy for the very same reason; and your obstetrician will take care of that. Your diet should be rich in greens, meat, green peas, dates etc. If you are anaemic, pregnancy will create more problems for you and thus for the baby as well.
- Build up calcium stores in your body by drinking plenty of milk, eating eggs, ragi etc and exposing at least your forearms and face to sun for at least 10 minutes every day between 9.00am and 3.00pm to improve vitamin D synthesis by your body. Vitamin D is very essential to maintain right calcium levels in your body. Your obstetrician would prescribe to you calcium and vitamin D tablets if deemed necessary. Most of the growth in baby's size occurs in the 8th and 9th months. So taking adequate calcium becomes all the more important at this stage so that the baby's bones grow well.
- Adequate diet is very important because you have to provide not for just yourself, but also your baby. You need to take 300 calories more than your pre-pregnancy diet provided you were taking adequate diet before conception. It will come to around 1 extra meal per day. Take good amounts of cereals, pulses/meat, eggs, milk, nuts, vegetables and greens in an easily digestible way.
- As I said before, any insult to the developing baby in the first 3 months will cause major defects in the baby. So avoid taking medicines on your own without consulting your doctor. Protect yourself from infections by practising strict hand washing and keeping away from congested places and infected persons i.e. those persons with fever, cough, cold, rash etc. Stay away from very hot objects and hot places. Do not bathe with very hot water. Stay away from alcohol, smoking and drugs. Stay away from X-rays, CT scan rooms etc. Consult your doctor immediately if you develop fever, rash, boils etc.
- Inadequately treated infection in you can spread to your baby both while in the womb, and during delivery. Whatever blood tests and other tests your doctor advises, get them done. These tests are necessary

to asses the status of your health and also to see if you are carrying any silent infections which can affect the growth and development of your baby.

- Some diseases like high blood pressure, diabetes (high blood sugar) and thyroid problems can also affect the baby adversely. Follow up with your obstetrician regularly to rule out such problems. Take necessary treatment in case you develop any such problems.
- Get ultrasound scans done as advised by your doctor. These are necessary to rule out defects and improper growth of your growing baby.

Rest adequately. Be happy and cheerful. All this will ensure proper growth of your baby.

Your ?s My Answers:

How are twins born?

Sometimes the fertilized egg (zygote) splits into two and grows into two babies. These babies will look identical and be of the same sex. Sometimes two eggs get fertilized at the same time by two different sperms and two babies develop in the womb at the same time. These babies may or may not be of the same sex and are not identical because they have developed from two different eggs.

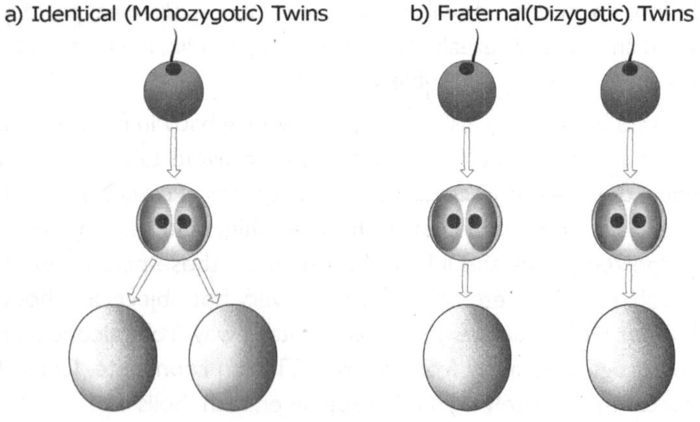

Fig: 4 Two different types of twin pregnancies

I am planning for my first pregnancy. My father has a disease because of which he bleeds into his knee joint often. Doctors told us that he has something called 'haemophilia'. What is the chance of my baby having the same problem? I am not having any such problem.

There is a chance of your baby developing the same disease or carrying the disease to the next generation without developing the disease. *It is always important to go for genetic counseling even before conception when histories of such diseases exist in the family.*

Why is it said that one should not marry a close relative?

Certain fatal and chronic diseases occur more commonly among the children of those parents who are closely related. It is better to avoid marrying a close relative because of this very reason.

I am planning for my first pregnancy. I have read about 'birthing centres' from western books. Are such services offered in Indian hospitals?

The 'cradle' is a concept modelled on birthing centres in the west. It aims at providing a home like environment, trained expertise throughout labour, excellent pain management, impeccable hygiene, antenatal as well as post natal classes and counselling, and the services of a lactation expert. The idea is to make the parents and the family go through the pregnancy, the birth of the baby and the post delivery period in a relaxed manner; and at the same time having the best of medical care available throughout. Such facilities are being made available in our country. In places like Banglore, 'the Cradle' concept has become a huge success.

❑❑❑

Things to be Kept Ready before the Arrival of the Newborn

- Baby blankets
- Baby mattresses (in case you plan to use a crib)
- Baby towels
- Diapers (non medicated and non perfumed)
- Wipes (non medicated and non perfumed)
- Cotton cloth pieces
- Bath sponges
- Cotton and gauze (for making cotton pads)
- Cotton balls (for wiping baby's eyes)
- Baby oil (olive oil, coconut oil etc – non-medicated and non-perfumed)
- Baby clothes
- Baby caps, socks, mittens/gloves
- Baby nail clipper
- Mosquito net
- Clean and well-ventilated room

Baby soap, baby shampoo etc are optional in the first few weeks. Nappy rash cream containing Zinc oxide can be purchased as and when necessary. Breast pump, baby sling, crib etc can be purchased as and when you want to start using them. Mother should purchase for herself those clothes which enable her to comfortably feed her baby.

❑❑❑

Section I

Zero to Six Months

Section I

1

Exclusive Breast Feeding

Let us first start with the most important thing for the baby's survival i.e. the baby's food. Mother's milk is the best food for the baby in all respects. Most mothers change over to formula milk/ cow's milk much earlier than what is recommended by paediatricians citing the reason that they do not have adequate milk for the baby. This is something which does not happen in the real sense provided the mother is well motivated and is happy to breast feed her baby. I hope that the following pages on 'exclusive breast feeding' will convince the mothers to practise the same.

Whenever baby suckles at the breast, certain hormones get secreted from a gland in the brain. These hormones stimulate the breast cells to produce and eject milk. One of these hormones helps the womb to go back to non pregnancysize and also makes the mother feel good and happy. Thus, frequent breast feeding not only ensures the best quality nutrition for the baby, but also helps the mother in bonding with the baby.

Your ?s My Answers:

What food should my diet consist of during the period of breast feeding?

You should take around 500 calories more than what you were taking before your pregnancy. It will come to around 2 extra meals per day. Milk should form a very important constituent of your diet. Take good amount of fluids (water, juices, butter milk, coconut water etc) and protein (dal, chicken, egg etc) so that you secrete good amount of milk. Make sure you take a good mixed diet consisting of cereals, milk, pulses/meat, fruits, nuts, vegetables and greens. Your doctor may advise you to take calcium, iron, vitamin and mineral supplements if deemed necessary. You should spend some time outdoors during the day time along with your baby so that she/

he gets adequate vitamin D; the synthesis of which is dependant on exposure to sunlight.

Some foods like nuts, peanuts, eggs, cow's/buffalo's milk, soya, fish, shell fish and wheat may produce allergy when secreted in breast milk; but it is rare to happen. Allergy can manifest as skin allergy, cough, cold and breathing problems, vomiting, diarrhoea (loose stools), blood in stools and excessive crying due to stomach pain etc. Here I would like to mention about some thing called 'infantile colic'.

- 'Infantile colic' is a condition where the baby cries incessantly in the evenings because of stomach pain. It causes a lot of anxiety to the mother. Allergenic foods in the mother's diet have been implicated. Inadequate burping also has been implicated. So it may help if you avoid allergenic foods in your diet and also burp your baby adequately so as to avoid the problem of 'colic'. A more detailed description of this condition is given in the following pages. It will be practically difficult to avoid foods like wheat, egg, and milk in your diet; but you can avoid them in the very rare case of your baby developing any of the above mentioned problems after you eat any of these foods.
- Also avoid too much of spice, coffee etc as these substances can also irritate baby's stomach. Most importantly, keep your spirits up and be happy to feed your baby so as to ensure good supply of milk to your baby.

It is advisable for the mother to be aware of all the facts that I have mentioned above so as to avoid problems for the baby. At the same time mothers shouldn't be paranoid about what they eat and compromise upon their food intake and nutritional status.

Should I avoid taking medicines during breast feeding? How do I protect my baby from harmful chemicals?

Some medicines used for treating thyroid problems and cancer are not supposed to be taken by mother during breast feeding. Some medicines like antibiotics may cause the baby to have diarrhoea. It is better that you take your doctor's advice before taking any medicines.

Some pesticides on fruits like grapes and some dyes in your clothing can be absorbed into your body and can be secreted in the milk. Similarly, industrial chemicals can contaminate the drinking water, and thus be secreted in the breast milk. Be aware of these facts and take proper precautions to avoid these problems.

What is the best food for the baby? Why?

Mother's milk is the best food for the baby. It contains all the essential nutrients for proper growth of the baby, and also protective factors which protect the baby against infections and allergies. The milk which is produced in the first 3-4 days is called colostrum. It is yellow in colour and rich in protein. It is very important for the baby as it contains protective factors which help the baby in fighting all the infections. Please do not deprive your baby of this benefit. It is very easy for the baby to digest mother's milk. Mother's milk is clean, uncontaminated, safe, and is at a temperature suitable for the baby. Mother's milk contains those substances which are good for the growth of baby's brain. Breastfed babies are less likely to be obese when they grow up. Generally, babies fed on cow's milk tend to sleep longer as their stomach gets emptier later. So there will be a tendency to give them cow's milk at nights. This needs to be avoided. Cow's milk will only add to the weight of the baby, whereas mother's milk has certain essential nutrients which are important for the development of brain. So I guess there won't be any doubt about whether you want your baby to be fat and dull or active and brainy! The baby feels happy, safe and secure; and thus the bonding between the mother and the baby is much stronger if the baby is exclusively breastfed. Exclusive breastfeeding helps the mother in remaining healthy; and the belief that it spoils her 'figure' is just a myth. Good support to the breasts is sufficient to prevent them from sagging. Exclusive breastfeeding also helps in contraception (birth control); though it is not a full-proof method.. Breast feeding is said to decrease the risk of breast cancer. Keeping in view the baby's and the mother's health; all the mothers should willingly and happily practise exclusive breastfeeding for the first four to six months; and start 'weaning foods' only after that period. It is recommended that breastfeeding be continued till two years of age in addition to other foods.

What do we mean by 'exclusive breast feeding'?

By 'exclusive breastfeeding' we mean that the baby should receive only mother's milk and nothing else; not even water for the first four to six months. Mother's milk is enough to take care of both the nutritional and fluid requirements of the baby. Giving any other fluid (including water) increases the chance of infection due to contamination.

When should breast feeding be initiated?

It is essential that breastfeeding be initiated within one hour of birth in case of a normal delivery and within 4 hours of birth in case of a caesarian delivery. Do not give sugar water etc to the baby. It will delay the establishment of lactation.

How and when to feed the baby?

This will be told to you by the child specialist when you are in the hospital. At home put the baby to your breast every 2-3 hours; and when the baby cries for feeds. Most of the babies finish their feed in the first 5-10 minutes itself; but some babies may take up to 15 minutes. If the breast has got emptied and the baby is still hungry, put the baby to the other breast. There will be a tight feeling at the base of the areola (the pigmented area around the nipple) when milk is being taken in by the baby. This kind of feeling won't be there once the breast gets emptied. Do not keep the baby at the breast for too long a time; otherwise he/she may swallow air and it may worsen the problem of 'colic' (there is a discussion about 'colic' in the following pages) and vomiting. You should not be too rigid about the schedule and the timing. The best way is to feed the baby on demand. Sometimes the baby may want to sleep for a longer time. At such times do not keep waking the baby up for feeds every 2-3 hours. You can wait up to 4 hours. The interval between two feeds should not be more than 4 hours in the new born period.

Why should the mother empty one breast first before putting the baby to the other breast?

The mother should empty one breast first before putting the baby to the other breast so that the baby gets all the hind milk (the milk which flows out last) which is more nutritious than the foremilk (the milk which flows out at the start).

Is it true that women with smaller breasts do not produce adequate milk for the baby?

No. Breast milk production predominantly depends on the mother's interest in feeding her baby; and the suckling of the breast by the baby. Worry, fear, stress etc suppress lactation. So try to be cheerful and happy to feed your baby in order to ensure good milk production.

Now..... how to hold the baby while feeding?

The mother can either lie down or sit comfortably and feed her baby. Make sure that the baby's head is at a higher level than the body. Feeding your baby should be a happy and satisfying experience. Many inexperienced mothers put just the nipple in the baby's mouth. This causes lot of discomfort and pain to the mother; and also the baby fails to get adequate milk. The baby should be held in such a way that around one inch radius of the areola (the dark brown area around the nipple) is in the baby's mouth. The areola shouldn't be scissored by the mother i.e. it should not be held tight between two fingers. Scissoring causes the milk outflow to be impeded. The baby's whole body should be facing the mother while feeding. Ensure that the nose does not get pressed against the breast; otherwise the baby will not be able to breath; and will start crying. All said and done; once the mother strokes the baby's cheek with her nipple, the baby fixes himself/herself at the mother's breast in the most suitable and correct position. The mother too gets acquainted with the whole process in a few days.

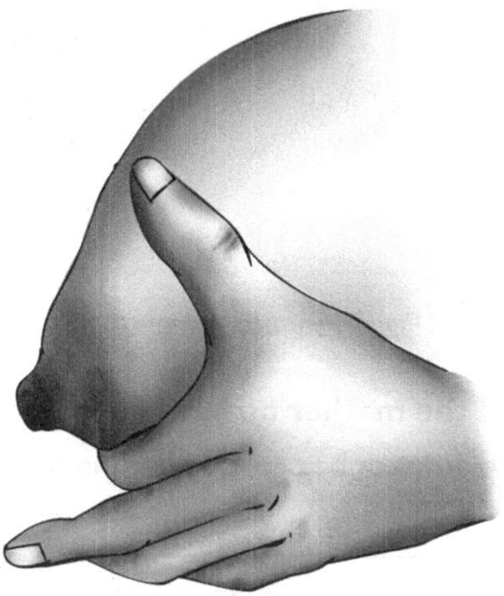

Fig:5 Holding the breast without scissoring

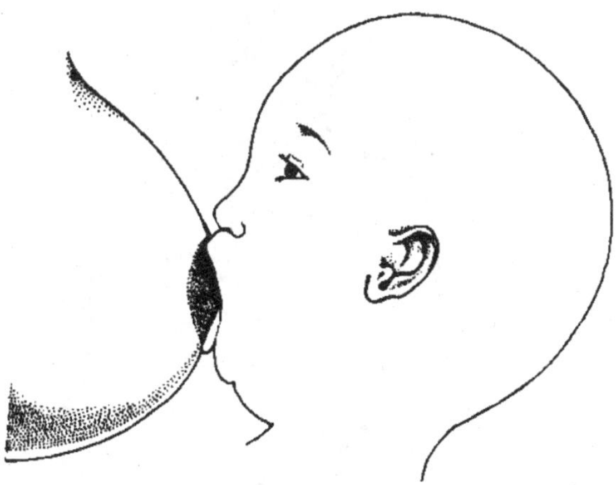

Fig: 6 Good attachment

Fig: 7 Poor attachment

What position should the mother be in while feeding the baby?

She can either sit, lie down or be propped up. She should feel comfortable while feeding the baby.

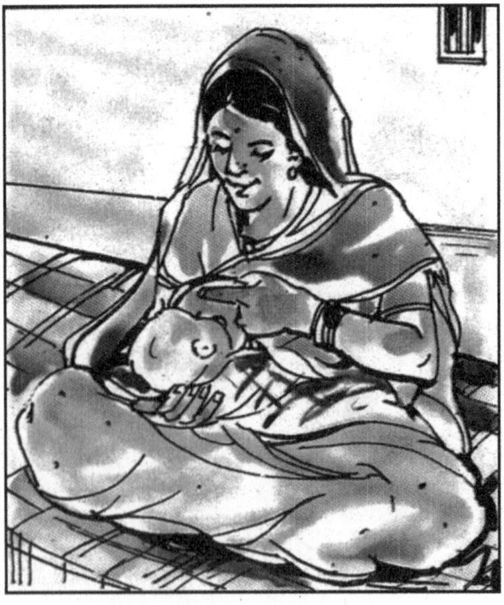

Fig: 8 Sitting and feeding the baby

Fig: 9 Lying down and feeding the baby

I find it difficult sometimes to release my baby from the breast. What can I do to make the process less painful?

Stroke the baby's cheek with your finger, gently insert your little finger into the baby's mouth from the corner of his/her mouth, and then gently release the baby from the breast.

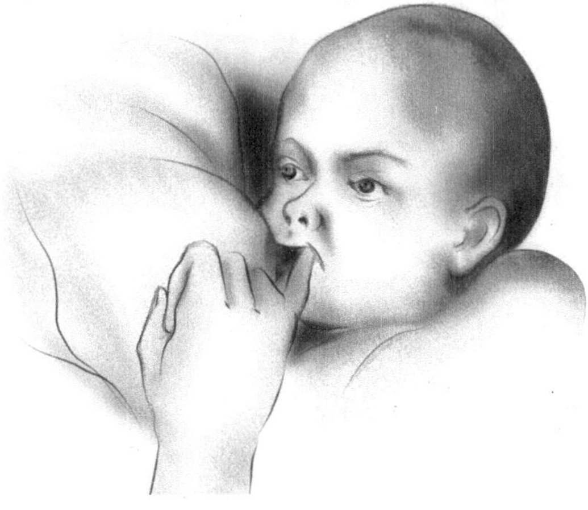

Fig: 10 Releasing the baby from the breast

How does the mother know if the baby is getting adequate milk?

If your baby sleeps comfortably after each feed, passes urine at least 6-8 times a day, passes stools with ease at least 1-2 times a day, is gaining weight adequately; then your baby is getting adequate milk. Many times when you feed the baby from one breast, milk dribbles down from the other breast as well.

What is 'burping'? Why should mothers do it? How should they do it?

Always remember to burp your baby after every feed. Burping is done to expel out the air that the baby would have swallowed during the feeding. Put the baby over your shoulder and gently pat the baby over the back till the baby burps. Ensure that the baby's head is well supported. Burping can also be done by laying the baby over your lap on his/her belly(making sure that the head is higher than the body, and also making sure that the head is well supported), and then gently patting the back till you hear the burping sound. You can also burp babies by seating them on your lap; supporting the head and chest with one hand from the front and gently patting the back with the other hand.

Fig: 11 (a) Burping your baby

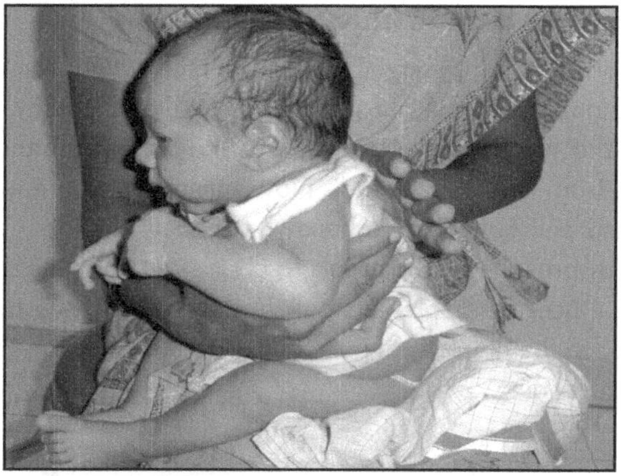

Fig: 11 (b) Burping your baby while sitting

Fig: 11 (c) Another technique of burping your baby

Many a time mothers complain to the doctor that their baby takes out milk after every feed. What can be done to avoid this?

This can be avoided to a large extent by the good practice of burping babies and placing them on their right side with the head end slightly higher than the rest of the body, or holding them upright for at least 10 minutes after every feed. Avoid changing nappies just after feeds because you would invariably put the baby on the bed and lift the lower part of his body. That would cause the milk to move up from the stomach and the baby would vomit. Sometimes overfeeding also can lead to this problem. This problem is more with formula feeds (especially when fed using bottles) than breast feeds. If the vomiting persists in spite of good feeding practices, do consult a child specialist.

My baby has hiccups after every feed. Is it normal?

Perfectly normal. Most babies tend to have hiccups after feeds.

What can be done if the mother has inverted nipples?

Try to correct them using the 'syringe technique'. You can use this technique to pull the nipple out just before feeding the baby. Take a 20ml syringe. Cut the 'nozzle end'. Now remove the piston from the 'piston end' and insert it from the 'nozzle end'. Now put the 'piston end' firmly over the areola and pull out the piston slowly to apply suction. Gently release the suction (by pressing on the areola to create gap between the areola and the syringe). Once the nipple gets pulled out, put the baby to your breast for feeding once the nipple gets pulled out. Do this regularly to pull out the nipples before feeding.

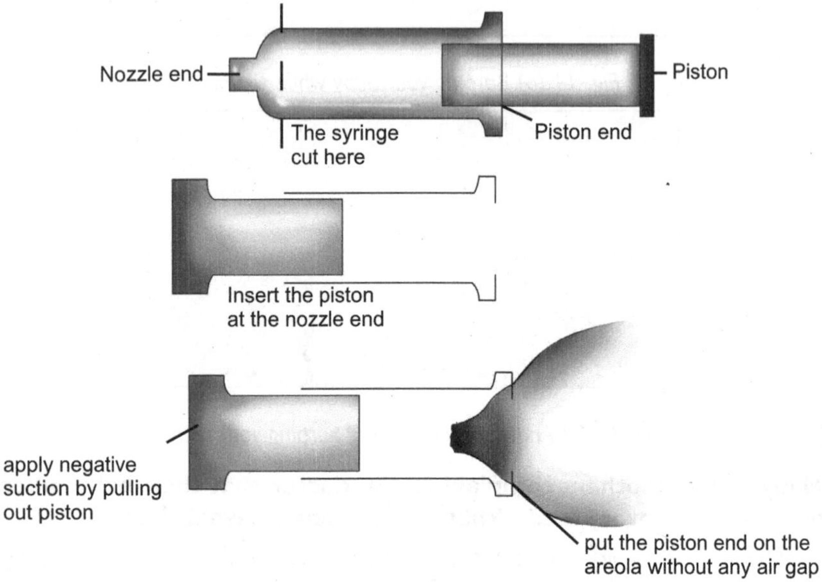

Fig: 12 Syringe technique

You can also try to use 'nipple shields' when you feed the baby. These nipple shields are made of silicone and have a small hole at the tip for milk to flow out. The suction pressure created in the nipple shield by baby's suckling will aid in free flow of the milk and also in keeping the nipple in extended position. Make sure you buy a nipple shield of the right size. Consult your doctor in case you are not able to correct your problem using either of these techniques.

What can be done to avoid engorgement of breasts?

Many a times mothers develop swelling and pain of the breasts due to accumulation of milk, especially if lactation is not established early and the baby is given top feeds (like sugar water, cow's milk, formula milk etc). Avoid this painful problem by initiating breast feeding early, and by practising exclusive breastfeeding as I have already told. Sometimes the mother may have cracked nipples, and thus avoid feeding the baby as it causes pain to her. In such a case apply 1 or 2 drops of the breast milk to the cracked nipples frequently so that they become supple and the cracks heal. Keep the nipples and the areolae clean and dry. Keep the nipples and the areolae soft and supple by massaging with coconut oil or vaseline. If feeding the baby is still causing pain, express the milk out and feed the baby with that milk, using a spoon. If you do not express the milk, you may develop painful swollen breasts which can get infected and pus may form in the breast. This will need hot fomentation (dipping cloth in warm water and applying it to the breasts), expressing out the breast milk, antibiotics and painkillers. Avoid such problems by following the simple instructions I have given you i.e. early initiation of breast feeding, exclusive breastfeeding, and expression of breast milk in case of cracked nipples and breast swelling. In case you develop fever and extremely painful breasts, it is better to consult a doctor.

How to care for the nipples?

Mother should start nipple care even before the birth of her baby. She should regularly apply coconut oil, vaseline or petrolatum emollient to the nipples and the areolae (the dark pigmented area around the nipples) regularly so that she doesn't develop nipple sores. Development of nipple sores can interfere with lactation, and so it is very important that proper nipple care be taken.

Now..... how to express the milk out?

You stroke firmly the breast from the base towards the areola from all sides at least a dozen times. Now support the breast with one hand and use the forefinger and thumb of the other hand to hold the breast tissue just behind the areola and press it against the base of the breast with a backward and slightly upward movement. Repeat this many times to express the milk out into a clean cup. You can repeat the entire process till you express sufficient milk. Wherever lumps are formed, apply hot fomentation and express the milk out as already told.

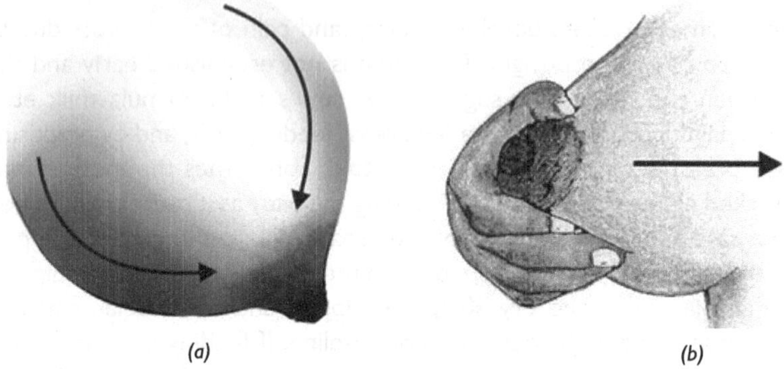

Fig: 13 (a) Stroking the breast before expression of milk
(b) Direction of force to be applied for expressing the milk

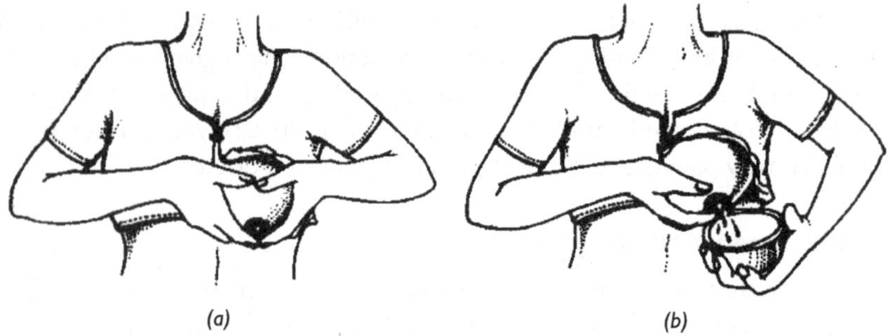

Fig: 14 A mother manually expressing her breast milk (a, b).

What are Breast Pumps? For what purpose are they used?

Breast pumps are mechanical devices that help the lactating mothers in expressing milk. They are available in medical shops, and shops which sell baby products. Both manually operated and battery/electricity operated pumps are available. They are quite expensive. In case you want to use less expensive devices; you can design your own breast pump using a 20ml syringe, and use it in the same way that I have described above for inverted nipples. Always ensure that the pumps, syringes and cups are sterilised by keeping them in boiling water for 10 minutes. Sterilisers (electricity operated) to do the same are also available in the market. Using them may make your job simpler.

I am a working mother. Many times milk oozes out from my breasts and causes me a lot of embarrassment in my work place. What can I do?

Try to empty your breasts periodically in the wash room. If it is feasible and there is a fridge in your office, you can try to collect the milk in a clean sterilised container for further use. Try using nursing pads. Change them frequently so that nipples and areolae remain dry and clean; otherwise you can develop fungal infection (thrush) in those areas. This 'thrush' can spread to the baby's mouth as well. Carry a spare shirt/ kurta with you, just in case your shirt/ kurta gets wet with the milk. Consult your doctor if you develop rash and itching in the areolae and the nipples.

Does the nutrition of preterm babies and low-birth weight babies differ from that of other babies?

Preterm (babies born more than 3 weeks before the due date) and small babies (less than 2.5 kg) require additional nutrients like protein, calcium, iron, vitamin E and zinc. Babies born in the ninth month generally do not need any additional nutrition other than mother's milk. They will be able to take milk directly from the breast. More premature babies will need to be fed with spoon initially. It is better to take your paediatrician's advice regarding how to feed the baby and about additional nutrients on an individual basis.

Is there any truth in the 'myth' that a mother cannot produce enough milk for 'twins'?

Another myth is that a mother cannot produce enough milk for twin babies. In fact, God has endowed the mother with the ability to produce enough milk even for twin babies. She can feed one baby first from one breast and the other baby afterwards from the other breast. She can also feed them simultaneously, holding one baby at each breast.

Many working mothers ask their doctor "how can I feed my baby exclusively on breast milk for 6 months? I will have to join work." What can be done in such a case?

Mothers can express the milk out, store it and use it to feed the baby by doing the following:

- Be sure to wash hands before starting to express the milk out.
- Use clean and leak proof containers.

- Breast milk can be kept at room temperature for 6 to 8 hours if room temperature is </= 25degrees Celsius. Covering the container with a cool cloth will help.
- Breast milk can be kept in an insulated cooler bag for 24 hours.
- Breast milk can be kept in the refrigerator for 5 days provided one keeps it well behind.
- Breast milk can be kept in the freezer for 2 weeks.

Take the stored milk out from the fridge around half an hour before so that it comes to room temperature before feeding the baby. To thaw frozen milk; put it in the non-freezer compartment of the fridge for some time, or hold the container under lukewarm water for 5-10 minutes. Once you bring the milk to room temperature, use it immediately or discard it. Never refreeze. Always bring the milk to room temperature before giving it to the baby. Never heat the milk to thaw it. Heating can cause uneven heating. Baby can get scalded and nutrient quality of the milk is affected by heating. Heating in the microwave can cause the container to explode.

Thus, even working women can continue feeding their babies with breast milk in their absence. The same applies for mothers who have to travel with their babies. The container containing breast milk can be kept in a pack containing ice cubes so that the milk doesn't get spoilt during the travel (insulated cooler bag).

How can mothers maintain adequate milk supply?

Mothers should be well motivated regarding breast feeding. Depression, worry, nipple sores, inverted nipples etc can interfere with lactation. Adequate care should be taken to prevent and correct such problems. Good diet, as had already been discussed, is important. Some allopathic and ayurvedic preparations help in increasing milk production; especially during the initial period of lactation. Ask your doctor about them. It is also believed that garlic increases the production of milk. Take good amounts of protein and fluids to improve the quality and quantity of milk.

Are there any contraindications to breast feeding?

Contraindications to breast feeding are very few. In general parents have to have a detailed discussion with the paediatrician regarding the absolute/ relative contraindications to breast feeding. Some contraindications to breast feeding are

(a) Mother is taking drugs for treatment of cancer.

(b) Mother has been administered radio iodine or other radio contrast agents.

(c) The baby is diagnosed with a condition called galactosemia.

If the mother has active tuberculosis or is HIV positive, the issues concerning breast feeding need to be discussed and managed on an individual basis by the paediatrician.

In this section I have tried to answer most of the queries regarding breast feeding. I hope that the mothers who read this book will have a better understanding about exclusive breast feeding and get motivated to exclusively breast feed their babies.

❑❑❑

2

Formula Food and Cow's Milk/Buffalo's Milk

Formula food is that food which is prepared artificially from cow's milk or soya protein in such a way that the food resembles the human milk as much as possible. They are available as milk powders. They are fortified with all the essential nutrients. Most of the formulae are cow's milk based. Formulae are available for babies 0 to 6 months of age, for babies from after 6 months till 1 year of age and for young kids 1 to 2 years of age. Milk can be prepared by adding these powders to boiled water by following the instructions given on the labels. It is advisable to avoid formulae at least in the first 6 months. I would like to re emphasize that **Mother's milk is the best food for the baby.**

In case you have to give formula milk to the baby for some reason, do follow the following tips to prepare it in the best possible way:

- Keep the lid tightly closed and do not use wet hands while taking the powder from the tin.
- Keep the tin in a cool clean place.
- Discard the tin if it crosses the expiry date.

Wash your hands thoroughly with soap and water and dry them before starting to prepare the formula milk.

- Use only the spatula given in the tin for measuring the milk powder.
- Follow the instructions on the label strictly to prepare milk of the right concentration. Generally most formulae are prepared in such a way that 1 spatula of powder needs to be added to one ounce (30 ml) of water. Boil water for 10 minutes after the bubbles appear. Cool it to being lukewarm before adding the milk powder. Shake the container well and ensure that no lumps of the powder remain in it.

- Many times too much powder is added to the water because the powder is stuffed into the spatula while taking the measured amount of milk powder. This can be avoided. Take a heapful using the spatula, move a clean dry knife across it so that the extra powder falls down and the powder is at level with the brim of the spatula. Do not shake the spatula in order to over stuff it with the milk powder.
- It is better to give formula milk using a spoon. In India for generations mothers have been using a spoon-like thing with a beak for giving milk and other fluids to the baby. It is more convenient than the spoon.

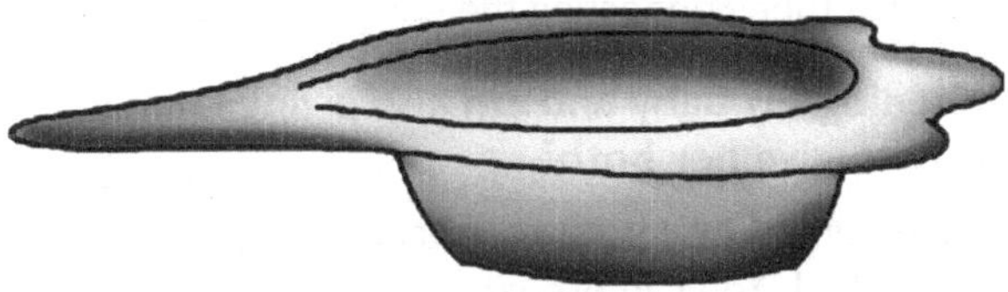

Fig: 15 Traditional Indian spoon for feeding babies

- In case you prefer to give formula using bottles, bottles have to be washed with mild liquid soap and then the soap has to be washed off thoroughly. Adding a drop of lemon or vinegar to warm water and rinsing the bottles will help. Sterilise the bottles for 10 minutes i.e. the bottles need to be boiled in the water for 10 minutes after water starts boiling. Bottles have to be held in such a way that the air remains at the back and the baby doesn't swallow the air. Stop feeding with the bottle when it is almost empty; otherwise baby will swallow air if you try to finish the milk till the last few ml. Never leave the baby alone with bottle in his/her hands.
- Nipples of the bottles have to be replaced periodically because they tend to become soft with repeated boiling. The nipple hole should be such that when you invert the milk bottle, milk should fall down at the rate of many drops per second after an initial thin stream. It should neither run down too fast like a continuous stream nor fall too slow like 1 or 2 drops per second. Always test the nipple using milk only, and not water. Do not shake the bottle when you are testing.

Your ?s My Answers:

We insist on using spoon, and not bottle for feeding the baby with formula milk. Why?

The chance of infection is much higher with bottle even if you boil the bottle and the nipples every day. The baby gets confused between the mother's nipple and the bottle's nipple; and this may create problems in restarting breast feeding. The chance of baby swallowing air and thus having 'colic' and vomiting is much more with bottle, especially when it is held in such a way that more air than milk goes into the baby's mouth. The problem of ear infection is also more with the bottle especially when the nipple hole is too big and the baby gulps down the milk. This is because some milk goes up into the ear via a tube connecting the ear to the area behind the nose.

I am breast feeding my baby and am also giving formula to her. What is the best way to give her both?

Breast feed her first. Once both your breasts are empty, you give formula till the baby is satisfied. You can prepare the formula milk and keep it ready before starting to breast feed her. If you have somebody to help you, then they can prepare the formula after you start feeding your baby.

How should the bottle be held while feeding the baby?

Hold it in such a way that air remains at the top and milk fills up the entire nipple. Stop feeding when the bottle is almost empty i.e. before the nipple becomes empty too; otherwise the baby will swallow a lot of air.

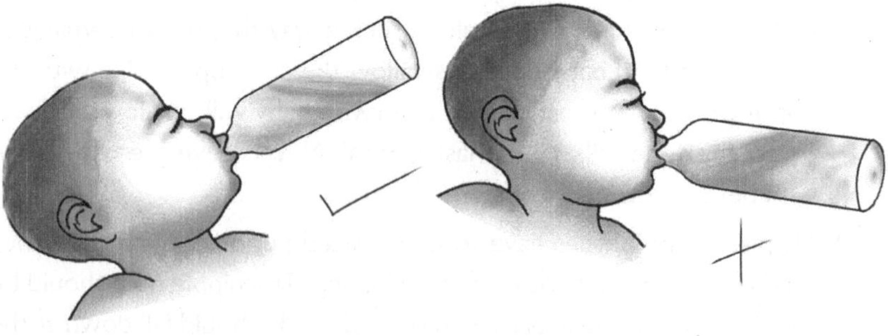

Fig: 16 The right and wrong methods of feeding the baby with the bottle

Keep removing the nipple from the baby's mouth periodically in order to release the vacuum. Thus, you will be ensuring free flow of milk into the baby's mouth. Otherwise the baby will suck in too much air and this will cause further problems as I have discussed already.

Why do doctors insist on avoiding cow's (or buffalo's) milk till one year of age?

I have already told you why mother's milk is the best milk for the baby. Now I will tell you how cow's milk can harm your baby. Cow's milk can cause constipation, can worsen dehydration (loss of water from the body). Cow's milk allergy can be very severe sometimes; and the baby goes on passing blood in stools. The loss of blood in the stools can cause anaemia (thinness of blood) and poor growth. Iron and certain other nutritional factors in cow's milk are not adequate for the baby. This can lead to anaemia and other problems. The chance of the baby developing asthma and other allergies in later life is more with cow's milk. It is better to avoid all these problems rather than waiting for them to occur, especially when it is in our hands to prevent them from occurring.

Why do doctors insist on avoiding formula feeds?

Doctors insist on avoiding formula feeds due to the following reasons:

- Chance of infection, diarrhoea (loose stools) and vomiting if not stored properly, or if water used is not boiled adequately.
- Chance of constipation and dehydration if adequate water is not mixed with the powder.
- Chance of diarrhoea if the baby is overfed with formula food.
- Chance of poor growth if too much water is added to the powder and the baby is underfed with formula food.

Moreover, formula feeds do not provide the immunity (protection) against infections that mother's milk provides to the baby. The chance of developing cow's milk allergy is always there because most of the formulae are prepared from cow's milk. Some formulae are prepared using Soya protein; but Soya allergy is also quite a common problem during this period.

How much milk needs to be given to the baby?

Around 5 to 6 ounces (1 ounce is equal to 30 ml) per kg body weight per day is the daily requirement. For example if a baby 2 months of age is weighing 4 kg; then the baby requires 20 to 24 ounces of milk in a day. You can feed the baby 6 to 7 times a day. In case you are giving cow's milk to the baby, you have to give her water in between (boiled and cooled water); otherwise there is a very high chance of the baby developing constipation, dehydration and excessive thirst. The baby will tend to become very irritable. Do not dilute the cow's milk; otherwise you may be compromising upon its caloric value and thus provide inadequate nutrition to your baby.

Which is better; cow's milk or formula milk?

Cow's milk is cheaper and more easily available. There is high chance of it getting spoilt if kept for longer duration; especially in summers. Formula food is costlier. There is less chance of contamination if it is stored properly. It is fortified with many essential nutrients in such a way that it comes closest to mother's milk in terms of digestibility and nutritional value. So if you can afford to buy formula, you are able to store it properly, and prepare it in the right way, I suggest you to use formula at least for the 1st year. If you cannot afford it, or you are not able to store it properly, or not able to prepare it in the right way; it is better to go for cow's milk. Always ensure that you use fresh cow's milk (you have to of course boil it and cool it to lukewarm temperature before giving it to the baby.)

Can I prepare the formula and keep it in the fridge for the next feed?

No. Formula milk once prepared should be discarded after 30 minutes. It will be clearly written on the label.

Do I have to add sugar to the formula or cow's milk?

Absolutely not. Adding sugar may in fact even cause diarrhoea.

3

Weaning

Weaning is the process of gradual introduction of solids into the baby's diet, and changing over from exclusive breast feeding to mixed diet.

It is one of the most difficult challenges faced by the mother. The baby will resist initially; and after a lot of 'trial and error' mother will be able to find out what suits her baby the best.

Your ?s My Answers:

When should weaning start?

Weaning should start between 4-6 months of age, preferably from after 6 months of age. Prior to this period, neither is the baby's digestive system mature enough to digest solid foods nor will the baby be able to swallow the solid foods without aspirating (food going into the wind pipe).

How do I start weaning my baby?

Start by giving a teaspoonful of rice water and gradually increase the quantity over a week. Weaning will be easier if you start by giving the rice water to the baby just before he/she is about to finish feeding from the breast. The time duration of that particular breast feed can be decreased as the quantity of the rice water is increased over a period of one week. At the end of one week, rice water should replace one regular breast feed of your baby. Skip one of the scheduled breast feedings and give rice water instead. Introduce dal water in a similar way in the following week. Gradually introduce other food items like mashed banana, mashed potato in a similar fashion. Gradually change from rice water and dal water to mashed rice and mashed dal. Fruits, greens and vegetables can be introduced in a similar fashion.

Do not add salt or sugar to the foods at least for the initial two months. one can start adding salt for taste to the baby's food once the baby starts drinking water on a regular basis. Adding too much sugar to the baby's food will make the baby have loose stools. Sometimes undigested fibre may appear in the stools. One mother actually thought that the 'banana fibres' were worms; and she brought the stool sample to my OPD for my opinion!!

Can I introduce egg now?

Do not introduce wheat, maize, egg white, cow's/buffalo's milk, soya, nuts, fish etc till one year of age. Egg yolk can be introduced at 9 months of age.

What other foods do I need to give my baby so that he gets a balanced diet?

Iron supplementation by giving greens, green peas, dates etc is important at this stage. Jaggery is also a good source of iron. Try adding it to some food items. Breast feeding is to be continued at the same time. Gradually introduce all the easily chewable foods in such a way that by 1 year of age, the child should be able to eat everything that you eat except for the very spicy and oily stuff. Go through the section on food and nutrition of children 6 months to 6 years of age for a better idea about nutrition and food habits.

Can I give my baby water?

Generally babies do not require water while on exclusive breast feeds. Now mothers can start giving water to drink once they start weaning their babies. One should start giving water with a cup or tumbler from around 6 months of age. The earlier the baby learns to drink from the cup, the better. Babies' water intake can be considered adequate if they are passing urine 6-8 times a day, and their stools are soft, and they sleep adequately.

Tell me something about 'ready to eat' baby food.

Baby food is also available in tins. It too is fortified with all essential nutrients. The same precautions as those followed for preparing formula milk have to be followed in preparing tinned baby food. Never try to give this type of food using a bottle. I believe that freshly prepared, easily digestible and balanced home food is better than tinned food. It is safer, healthier and more appetising.

What is food fortification?

Addition of various essential nutrients to foods in the right amounts to improve their nutritional quality is known as fortification. Formula milk and other baby food are fortified with various nutrients. Similarly, salt is fortified with iodine to prevent deficiency of thyroid hormone. Nowadays fortified attas, which are fortified with various vitamins and minerals, are also available.

❑❑❑

Digestion and Excretion

Digestive system of a newborn is immature. It matures gradually as the baby grows up. Any insult to it in the form of early introduction of solid foods, early introduction of allergenic food items like eggs and peanuts can cause multiple problems like loose stools, vomiting, stomach pain etc. Similarly a newborn's intestine is less resistant to infections; and so there is more chance of diarrhoea and vomiting even with minimal contamination of food. ***Remember that mother's milk is uncontaminated and safe for the baby.*** Stool consistency and frequency change as the baby grows up. The type of food given to the baby plays a very important role in determining the stool frequency and consistency. Inexperienced mothers tend to worry about these changes even if the baby looks well otherwise. In this section, I tried to address some such apprehensions regarding baby's digestion and excretion. Doubts regarding introduction of solid foods and introduction of allergenic foods have been discussed in the previous sections.

Your ?s My Answers:

My baby passed blackish green coloured stools initially. Now she is five days of age. She is passing loose yellowish stools after every feed and I am worried that she may lose water from her body because of the diarrhoea. Should I give her some medicine?

No. Babies pass blackish green coloured stools initially. 3-5 days later, the stools gradually thin out and become more yellowish in colour. During this period, babies pass loose stools frequently, and sometimes after every feed. This phase lasts for a few days before the stool consistency improves and the frequency comes down. All babies go through this phase, and your baby is no exception. You need to worry only if your baby is not active, is passing urine less frequently than before, has dry mouth, eyes appear sunken, or has fever. It is better you consult a doctor in such a case.

When does a newborn pass stools?

Most of them pass meconium (stools of a newborn) within 48 hours. Any further delay in passing meconium needs to be looked into by a paediatrician.

My baby girl is passing excessive flatus (gas). What can I do?

Do not worry about it if it is not causing any discomfort to your baby. Burp her adequately. Make sure that she attaches well to your breast while feeding so that she doesn't swallow much air. Avoid bottle feeds, because the chance of swallowing air is more with bottle feeding. Also try to avoid allergenic foods, spices etc in your diet.

My baby is 3 weeks of age. She passes stools once in 3 days. I am worried.

Many breast-fed babies pass stools infrequently for a few weeks, especially after the first 2-3 weeks of life. The mother has nothing to worry about as long as the stools are soft and non bulky; the baby is comfortable, is passing flatus (gas) normally, has no distension of the stomach, is not vomiting greenish or foul smelling material, is feeding well, and gaining weight adequately. Do get a paediatricians's opinion (sometimes there may be a need to rule out thyroid and other problems). This infrequency of stools doesn't occur with formula feeds. In case it occurs, get a paediatrician's opinion.

My baby is 3 weeks of age. He is passing small amounts of dark green stools frequently. He is not gaining weight adequately. What might be the problem?

Your baby is not being fed adequately; and therefore he is having what we call as 'starvation stools'. Start feeding him adequately and weight gain needs to be monitored strictly. Consult your paediatrician.

My baby is 6 months of age. I have started weaning him at 5 months of age. He is passing hard pellet like stools. He strains a lot while passing stools. What can be done?

High protein content (e.g. too much of dal), low water content, and low fibre (fruits and vegetables) content in his diet can cause constipation. Increase the water and fibre content in his diet. Pureed fruits will definitely help. Some types of bananas can cause constipation. You can try giving some other types of bananas which suit your baby, and do not cause constipation.

Soak few dry grapes and dry dates in water over night, and give her few spoons of that water to drink in the morning. It will help her in having softer stools. Consult a paediatrician if his constipation doesn't improve with the above measures.

My baby is 2 days of age. She passed blood in her stools yesterday. What might be the reason?

Are you having cracked nipples? In that case, your baby might have swallowed blood from them while feeding. Has she received vitamin K injection at birth? If not, she might be bleeding due to deficiency of vitamin K. She might even be bleeding from some raw area near the anus. In any case she needs to be examined by a paediatrician; and some tests on her stools and possibly blood may have to be done to figure out the cause. The treatment will be given accordingly.

When does a newborn baby pass urine?

A newborn baby passes urine within 12 to 24 hours after birth. The paediatrician needs to be informed if the newborn baby doesn't pass urine within 24 hours after birth.

❑❑❑

5

Growth and Development

All three growth parameters i.e. head circumference, weight, height are plotted regularly on the growth chart by the paediatricians. Any deviation from the normal pattern would be recognized by the paediatrician and would be addressed to immediately. Nutrition is the most important factor which determines growth at this age. Generally birth weight doubles by around 5 months of age. It becomes 4 times the birth weight by one year of age. Similarly height becomes double of the birth length by 4 years of age. All these are just approximations. Finally a normal growth curve (on the growth chart) is the most important factor which will tell you that your baby is growing appropriately.

Incase of premature babies, time allowance for catch up growth is 1 ½ years for head circumference , 2 years for weight and around 3 to 3 ½ years for height; i.e they generally catch up with their peers by this age.

Babies will start smiling at the mother (social smile) at around one and half months of age, a very beautiful moment for the mother.

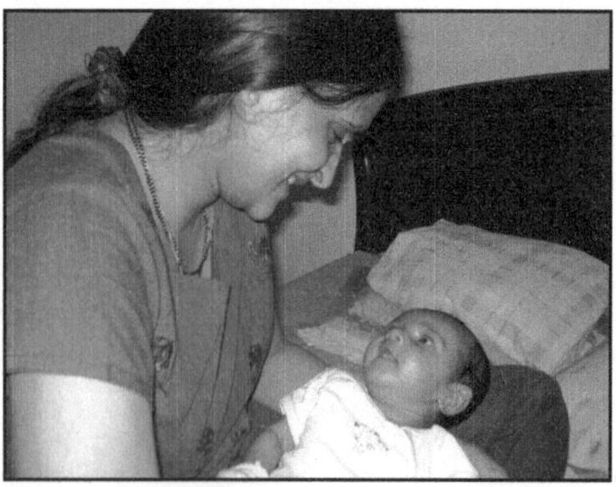

Fig: 17 Social smile

They will develop adequate head control by around 3 to 4 months of age. Babies will be able to support themselves on their forearms by around 12 weeks. They will start cooing and laughing by around 3months of age. Babies will usually roll back on to their stomach between 4 and 6 months. Get ready with your camcorder to record this achievement of your baby.

Fig: 18 After rolling over

By six months they will usually be able to sit supporting themselves on their hands.

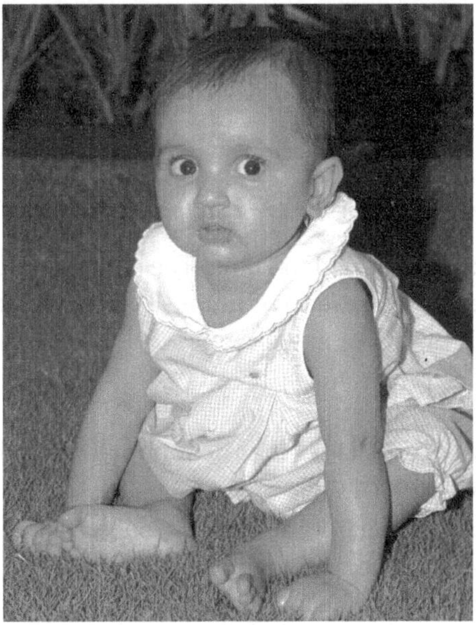

Fig: 19 Sitting with support

Baby will start reaching out for the rattle at around 4-5 months of age, will start taking it to the mouth by 5-6 months of age, and will be able to transfer it to the other hand by around 6 months of age. It is real fun to watch babies doing this.

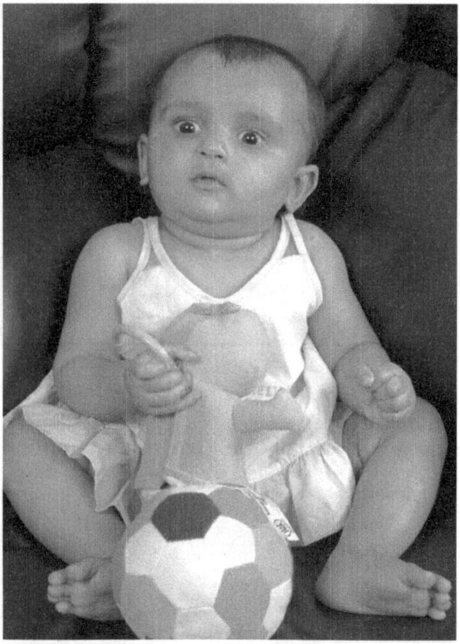

Fig: 20 After transferring the toy from the left hand to the right hand

Babbling will start at around this time. Their 'ma's and 'ba's are real music to the mother's ears. You have to treasure all these mile stones.

Your ?s My Answers:

My baby is 7 days of age. I feel that he looks thinner than what he was at birth. I am very worried.

Nothing to worry about. All babies lose around 10% of their birth weight in the first one week of life; and then regain it by 10 – 14 days of life. After that, they gain around 20- 30 g /day in the first 3 months of life, and 15- 20g/ day in the next 3 months. As long as your baby is gaining weight consistently, is active, and passing urine and stools normally, you have nothing to worry about.

How often do I have to weigh my baby girl?

Once a day in the 1st few days till discharge from the hospital. Text books say that you should weigh every week for the first 2 months, every month after that till one year of age and every 6 months after 1 year of age. It is practically difficult to do that. Weigh the baby every day till discharge from hospital. Weigh again after one week. After that, it would suffice to weigh her during vaccination visits unless your paediatrician advises you to get her weighed more frequently for some reason.

My baby is 5 months of age. She looks smaller than babies of her age. She was born 7 weeks before my due date. Her birth weight was 1.4 kgs. Will she catch up with other babies?

Yes. She will catch up with other babies in due course provided she gets good nutrition. Generally 'very low birth weight babies' (babies weighing less than 1.5 kg) catch up with other babies in terms of weight by around 2 years of age and in terms of height by around 3 to 3 ½ years of age.

❑❑❑

6

Cry and Pain

It is a common scenario in a clinic to see mothers telling the paediatrician that their babies cry excessively at night, or keep crying all the time. Many a times it is very difficult for the paediatrician to allay their anxieties. Most of the time babies cry due to hunger, sleepiness or due to some discomfort. 'Infantile colic' is one of the commonest causes for excessive crying of the baby in the early months. A Mother, with experience, will gradually learn to identify why her baby is crying and will learn to tackle the problem accordingly. In case the baby is inconsolable in spite of all your endeavours to console him/her, it is necessary to get a paediatrician's opinion to rule out serious problems.

Your ?s My Answers:

My baby is 3 weeks of age. She is crying excessively for the past one week; especially in the evenings. She pulls up her legs on to her tummy while crying, and she is inconsolable. I get very anxious when she cries inconsolably like this. I feel that she is in severe pain; possibly stomach pain. What should I do?

The condition described by you is something called 'infantile colic', which has it's onset at 2 weeks of age, peaks at 6 weeks of age and usually subsides by 4 months. It is said that colic is due either to air accumulating in the stomach, or to allergy to some food items in the mother's diet. So far none of the medicines used proved very effective. Many drugs are available in the medical shops for treating colic (simethicone, dill seed oil, fennel oil, phenergan etc). Phenergan can cause the baby to sleep too much, and an overdose is dangerous. Other medicines also have not proved to be very effective in treating colic, though some mothers report benefit with preparations containing simethicone. The best way in my opinion is to burp your baby after every feed. If the colic appears to be temporally related to certain foods in your diet, avoid them. Also understand that this is a common problem, and that your baby is not suffering from any serious condition. Do not give 'gripe water' etc and cause further problems for the baby. Gripe water is an alcoholic preparation and does help some babies in relieving abdominal discomfort, but can also cause harmful side effects like diarrhoea and loss of water from your baby's body.

My baby is 4 weeks of age. I feel she cries excessively, almost 3 hours a day. Is it okay?

Normally babies cry up to 2-3 hours a day (maximum at 6 weeks of age). By around 3 months of age it comes down to 1 hour a day. They usually cry when they are hungry, when they pass urine or stools, when they feel uncomfortable due to the heat or cold, when ants etc bite them, due to stomach pain, due to loneliness or due to uncomfortable clothing. Here I would like to emphasise that mothers should not try to feed the baby every time the baby cries, but instead try to find out why the baby is crying. They should tackle the problem accordingly. Do get a paediatrician's opinion if the baby becomes inconsolable.

Why does my baby cry before passing stools?

Most babies do that. Do not worry as long as he is not constipated and is not straining hard to pass stools.

Can I make my baby suck at a pacifier to keep her quiet?

I would not prefer you to do that. Try to find out why she is crying, and tackle the problem accordingly. Spend more time with her. Give her adequate breast feeds. The more secure a baby feels, the less the need for a pacifier. Pacifier itself may create some problems. She may swallow more air, and thus it may worsen her colic. She will vomit out her feeds if she swallows too much air. It may become difficult to wean her off the pacifier in future. Imagine her running around with the pacifier in her mouth at 1 year of age!!!!!!

❑❑❑

7

Sleep

Babies sleep around 15-17 hours a day in the newborn period. Some mothers even complain that their baby seems to be always sleeping except when he/she wakes up for feeds. In the first few weeks breast-fed babies wake up almost every two to three hours for feeds. The mother has to learn to cope up with the stress of having her sleep interrupted every 2-3 hours.

Your ?s My Answers:

When do the babies start sleeping for longer periods at night?

By 2-3 months of age, most babies start sleeping for 4-6 hours at a stretch during nights. Mothers should avoid stimulating and talking to the babies when they wake up during night time for feeds. Avoid bright lights at night when the baby is sleeping. Let the baby be in well-lighted areas when awake. This will help the baby in sleeping for longer time at nights and developing day night discrimination. Otherwise you will also have to join the elite club of mothers who complain that their baby stays awake at nights and sleeps during the day. Most babies develop day night discrimination by 1 ½ to 3 months of age.

Keeping a diary to record the baby's daily feeding schedule and napping schedule will help the mother to plan things better. Thus, she will feel less stressed.

Where should mothers put the baby to sleep? What precautions are to be taken to avoid accidental suffocation?

Babies regulate their temperature and breathing better when they sleep close to the mother; but there is a chance of accidental suffocation if the mother accidentally rolls over on to the baby. The chance of accidental suffocation of the baby is more if the bed is too small. Try to put the baby to sleep in the same cot as the mother, provided the cot is spacious and one can be sure about not rolling over on to the baby. If one cannot be sure about it, it is better to put the baby to sleep in a crib in the same room as the mother. The crib should be clean and comfortable. At the same time soft pillows, soft toys, sharp objects, and ropy materials should not be kept in the crib; otherwise there is a chance of suffocation, injuries and entanglement. Baby should be kept warm with adequate clothing as I have described in the subsequent sections. Baby should be put to sleep on her/his back, and not on the tummy; otherwise the chance of accidental suffocation is very high.

My baby keeps waking up at night. Is it normal for him?

Yes. Generally newborns sleep for 15-17 hours. They keep waking up every 2-3 hours for feeds and sleep again after sometime. Most mothers feel anxious about their baby waking up at night; but it is nothing to worry about. By the time your baby is 2- 3 months of age, the night time crying will come down. Till then mother has no choice but to cope up with the stress of waking up frequently at night. Some babies may continue to wake up 2-3 times at night even up to 2 years of age in spite of adequate feeds. Avoid uncomfortable clothing, use good quality diapers, protect him from mosquitoes, ensure comfortable sleep environment in addition to adequate feeds. You should also learn the art of falling asleep as soon as the baby dozes off; otherwise lack of sleep will start taking its toll on you and your baby as well.

Put your baby in bed once he is drowsy and allow him to fall asleep all by himself. You can rock him or sing to him till he feels drowsy. Generally all babies wake up a few times at night. They will comfort themselves back to sleep provided you stick to the routine of putting them in the bed when they are drowsy. If you rock them, feed them, or sing to them till they go into deep sleep; they will expect you to do the same to put them back to sleep when they wake up at night. That will cause your sleep to be disturbed and your baby will continue to associate his sleep with the same process of rocking, feeding, or singing. It will be difficult to wean him away from that habit later on. 'Prevention is better than cure'. Isn't it?

What is swaddling?

New born babies have many unwanted movements which disturb their sleep. They get startled frequently even while sleeping. Swaddling is the processes of bundling up the baby in a comfortable cloth in such a way that the baby's unwanted movements are minimised and the baby sleeps comfortably. This can be done up to an age of one and half to two months after which the baby's movements should not be restricted. Anyway babies will not like being swaddled after this age. Some babies may not like to be swaddled. In that case, you should leave them alone or try swaddling only the lower part of the body. Use a soft cotton cloth for swaddling. Ensure that the baby doesn't feel hot and stuffy inside it.

How do I swaddle my baby?

Take a soft cotton cloth. Spread it on the bed in the shape of a diamond. Fold the top corner down a little bit and put your baby on it in such a way that the neck rests on the folded part. Take the right corner and fold it over the straightened right arm and the trunk and tuck it under the back on the left side. Take the bottom corner and fold it over the legs and trunk and tuck it under the right shoulder. Lastly, take the left corner over the straightened left arm and the trunk and tuck it under the back on the right side.

❑❑❑

8

Temperature Regulation and Clothing

Keeping the baby warm (neither hot nor cold) and clothing the baby appropriately is an important aspect of baby care. Many a time babies are brought to the emergency cold, pale and gasping just because they weren't clothed adequately. It is also not very uncommon to see mothers bringing babies to the hospital saying that the toes have become blue; and this time the culprit is the tight sock that the mother has put on the baby's foot. Mothers also tend to misinterpret slight warmth as fever and thus tend to panic. Some of these common problems related to temperature regulation and clothing of the baby have been discussed here more in detail.

Your ?s My Answers:

How should mothers clothe their babies so that the baby keeps warm?

Keeping the baby warm (neither hot nor cold) is very important. If the room temperature is 27 degrees centigrade or more, the baby can do with a T shirt and shorts. Please use cotton shirts in summer. Use 'cotton-woolen mix' clothes in winter. The baby's clothes should be in such a way that they are easy to put on, and easy to remove. The baby will need extra layers of clothing in case the temperature is below 27 degrees centigrade. The baby needs to be covered with a blanket and will require head cap, socks, and gloves in addition to 2 layers of clothing in case the room temperature is below 20-21 degrees centigrade. Do not use tight socks and gloves. Many a time they are so tight that they impede the blood flow to the feet and hands; thus causing pain. Sometimes, such mistakes can prove to be fatal (some babies had to even get their toes amputated). During summers, take care that babies are in a cooler place. Otherwise they may develop fever, dehydration and other problems. ***Preterm babies tend to find it more difficult to maintain their body temperature.*** One has to be extremely vigilant when caring for a preterm baby and take all the necessary measures to ensure that the baby is kept warm.

How do mothers know that their baby is keeping warm?

Feel your baby's body, hands and feet. In case the hands and feet are cold, or if they appear pale or blue; you should understand that the clothing is inadequate .Do not keep your baby near the window, or very close to a fan especially if cold wind is blowing.

What should mothers do if their babies develop fever?

Sometimes you may feel that the baby is hotter than usual. Feel the body, hands and feet. If you feel that the entire body is hot, it may be due to the environment being hot, or it may be due to inadequate feeds. In such a case, keep the baby in a cooler environment and increase the feeds. If the fever persists for longer than an hour, then do get a paediatrician's opinion. If the baby feels very hot, or if the hands and feet feel cold when the body is feeling hot, do get a paediatrician's opinion. The baby might have developed fever due to some infection.

How should the baby's clothes be?

Baby's clothes should preferably be made from natural fabric. They should be soft, comfortable, clean, and easy to put on and remove.

I have a baby 5 months of age. I dress him so much that he sweats even in winters. In spite of that he catches cold in winters as well as in summers. How do I avoid this problem?

Firstly, do not overdress your baby thinking that you are going to protect him from cold by dressing him like that. Common cold is caused by viruses circulating in the environment. Good hand washing, keeping the house clean, dust free, dry and well ventilated , and dressing him to keep him warm and comfortable will help you in protecting him from cold. Keep him away from crowded places. Get the air coolers/ air conditioners serviced regularly in summers. Boost his immunity by exclusively breast feeding him till 6 months of age, continuing breast feeds till 2 years of age, and giving him a balanced diet once you start weaning him. Do not overdress him and make him feel hot and sweaty.

❑❑❑

9

Skin, Scalp and Hair

In the hospital, the temperature of the baby is stabilised first, and then blood etc are removed from the face, neck, and from the genital area using sterile cotton sponge and sterile water. Once the baby is comfortably maintaining his/her temperature, you can give the baby a bath. Do not try to forcibly remove the sticky white material sticking to the baby. It gets removed in one or two days by sticking to the baby's clothing. Let the water you use for the baby's bath not be cold (water can be at room temperature in summers, or slightly warm during other seasons).

Following are some Do's and Don'ts while taking care of your baby's Skin, Scalp and Hair:

- **Cleaning:** The soap should be low alkaline baby soap (it will be written on the soap cover). Anyway, baby soaps are available in all the medical shops and shops selling baby products. Thorough cleaning with clean boiled and cooled water using a clean sponge is good enough. Soap is not a must. If your baby weighs less than 2 kg, wait for at least one week before using soap. Always clean the face with water and sponge. Do not splash water over the face. Do not use soap on the face. Take care that water doesn't go into the eyes, mouth, nose, and ears while bathing the baby. Always support the baby's head while bathing the baby. Use cotton soaked in water (or disposable non medicated baby wipes) to clean the area when baby passes stools or urine. Do it gently, and from front to back so that the stool matter doesn't come in contact with the other genital areas.
- **Massaging:** Oil massage to the baby's skin is a good practice. Oil protects the baby's skin from the loss of moisture and heat. It not only keeps the baby's skin soft and supple, but also helps in establishing a better bond between the mother and the baby (the baby too feels

good the same way you or I would feel good with an oil massage). You can use olive oil or coconut oil for the massage. Massage should be given in such a way that the baby enjoys it. Be gentle. There is no need to apply the traditional mixture of basin, turmeric and atta for the massage. People do it because it removes the hair on the baby's body. The hair on the newborn's body will anyway fall irrespective of whether you apply this mixture, or not for the massage. Neither is this flour mixture going to stop your baby from developing new hair on the body. In fact, some babies may even develop skin rash secondary to it.

- **Don'ts:** Make sure that oil is not instilled into the eyes, nose, ears and mouth. Do not apply medicated creams and ointments to the baby without doctor's advice. Sometimes these creams get absorbed into the body and can cause serious problems, especially in the case of preterms. Avoid applying 'kajal' to the eyes as it will irritate the baby's eyes and sometimes damage them.
- **Moisturising:** Apply good amount of baby cream (non-medicated and non- perfumed) to the baby's skin, especially during winters. Apply the cream just after bath when the skin is still moist, as this will keep the baby's skin soft and supple through out the day. Always apply a small amount of cream over arms or legs initially to make sure that the cream suits the baby's skin, and doesn't produce any allergic rash. Once you are satisfied that the cream suits your baby's skin, you can apply it liberally as I have said before.
- **Powdering:** Applying too much powder (what many mothers do; especially in summers) is not good for the baby's skin. Powder particles will block the sweat pores and may cause pimple like rash over the baby's body. It is better to apply powder only to the neck, under the arms, in the groins and other body folds where friction is likely to be more.

Your ?s My Answers:

My newborn baby's hands look blue. Otherwise he is fine. What can be the problem?

There is no problem. It is the same with all newborns in the first few days.

My baby is having greenish to grayish black patches on the back and buttocks. Will they disappear with time?

These patches are called 'mongolian spots'. They are present in many babies. They tend to disappear by 1 year of age. Rarely they may persist up to 2-3 years of age.

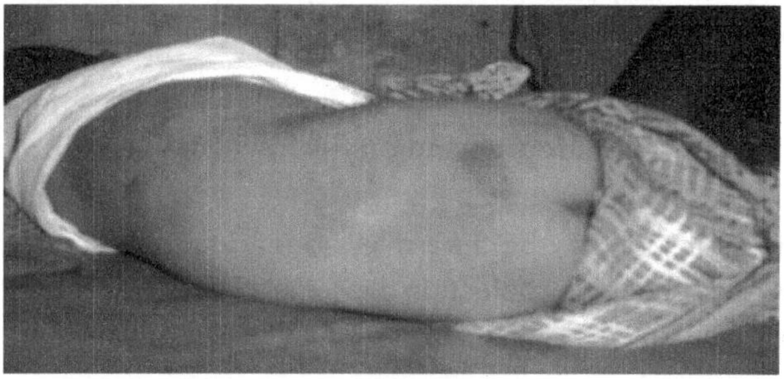

Fig: 21 Mongolian spots

My baby has pearl like white things on the face, especially near the nose and on the cheeks. What are they?

They are called 'milia'. They will disappear in a few weeks time.

My baby is 4 days of age and has small red-coloured patches all over the body. Some of them have a yellow tip. Should I worry about them?

They commonly occur in many babies on the 2nd or 3rd day of life, and disappear by one week. Nothing to worry about. If the lesions are too big and yellow, or your baby looks unwell, then get a paediatrician's opinion. In medical terms, the condition is known as 'erythema toxicum'.

My baby is 4 weeks of age. He developed a red pimply rash on his face. What can be done?

Your baby has developed 'infantile acne'. This will disappear in a few months time. Do nothing more than cleaning his face with gentle baby soap once or twice a day. Do not aggravate the problem by applying creams or lotions over the rash. Always take your doctor's advice. Do not poke the lesions with pins etc. If the lesions look too big and red with yellow tips, consult a paediatrician immediately as they might have got infected.

My baby has a reddish purple lesion on the left side of her face. What do I do about it?

Such lesions in newborn period need careful evaluation. Many are transient, whereas some tend to grow bigger and are associated with various other eye related problems, fits etc. Do follow up with the paediatrician.

My baby has a big mole on her back. Is it anything to worry about?

Some such lesions do no harm; and some can later become cancerous. The presence of many such lesions also may be a pointer towards problems in the future, especially those related to brain and nerves. Careful evaluation is needed.

My baby has a pit like depression on his lower back. Is it of any problem?

Sometimes it just may be a harmless one; but sometimes it may be a pointer towards underlying defects in the spinal cord. It needs to be evaluated by a paediatrician.

My baby is I month of age. Recently she developed a reddish lesion on her face which is increasing in size. What do I do about it?

Leave the decision to the doctor. Many such lesions resolve on their own as the child grows older.

My baby has slight peeling of her skin on the hands and feet. She is 3 days of age. What should I do?

Peeling of skin, especially on the hands and feet in the initial few days is normal. Nothing to worry about. Give nice oil massage to your baby.

My baby has developed yellowish scales over the scalp. Is it some kind of fungal infection?

No. This is something called 'cradle cap'. It will disappear by itself in a few weeks. Applying olive oil with 2% salicylic acid, and shampooing with 'baby shampoos' will hasten the removal; but it is always important to take a paediatrician's opinion at least once.

My baby is I month of age. She has lost all her hair at the back of her head. I am very worried.

Don't worry. It is common with many babies. The hair is going to grow back.

My baby seems to have lot of hair on her body. She was born a few days back. What do I do to get rid of that?

You don't have to do anything. The hair is going to disappear by itself in due course.

❑❑❑

Diapers and Diaper Rash

Many babies develop diaper rash (any rash in the diaper area). This can easily be prevented from occurring. Avoid using diapers when at home. Keep the genital area dry always, and let it get some air. Prepare soft cotton pads using cotton and gauze (in the shape of a square), and put them under the baby's buttocks when at home. Dispose them off when they get soiled. It is easier to keep the genital area clean and dry this way rather than by using diapers. Use wet cotton or a soft wet cotton cloth soaked in water (or disposable non medicated baby wipes) to clean the area when baby passes stools or urine. Do it gently, and from front to back so that the stool matter doesn't come in contact with the other genital areas.

Your ?s My Answers:

What kind of diapers should I use for my baby?

Use good quality disposable diapers or clean cotton cloth diapers which fit the baby snugly. The disposable diapers should be made of absorbent gelling materials (AGMs), be non-medicated, have good absorbent capacity, and be soft. Washing the cloth diapers, rinsing them thoroughly off the soap, washing them once more in dettol, and drying them in bright sunlight will help to prevent rash and infection in the diaper area.

What do I do if my baby develops 'diaper rash'?

In case your baby develops diaper rash, consult a paediatrician. Applying Zinc oxide cream or a petrolatum emollient twice a day, keeping the area dry and frequent change of diapers would help in case the baby has already developed diaper rash. In case the rash is suggestive of fungal infection, your paediatrician would prescribe the appropriate treatment. It is necessary to consult the paediatrician when your baby develops 'diaper rash'. Sometimes the rash can get infected. This infection can easily spread into the blood and other parts of the body and endanger the life of the baby. Therefore it is imperative to treat it early and in an appropriate manner.

What precautions should I take when I put diapers for my baby at night?

Ensure that you use good quality diapers for your baby. Change the diaper at least once at night. Apply good amount of Vaseline in the diaper area before putting on the new diaper.

❑❑❑

11

Baby Bath

Baby bath is something which you have to acquaint yourself with. Always learn the technique from more experienced mothers before venturing out on your own.

For the initial few days i.e. till the umbilical cord dries up and falls, give only sponge bath i.e. clean the baby with a clean sponge/soft cotton cloth. Use a clean sponge/soft cotton cloth soaked in warm water for this purpose. It is preferable not to use soap and shampoo for the first few weeks. In case you want to use soap and shampoo, make sure that they are low alkaline. It is preferable to delay the use of soap and shampoo further in case your baby is a preterm baby (baby born more than 3 weeks before due date).

keep the following things at hand and ready before you give bath to your baby:

- A baby bath tub
- Soft towels
- Clean sponge/soft cotton cloth
- Cotton balls
- Baby soap
- Baby shampoo
- A set of clean clothes and a clean nappy
- Lukewarm water

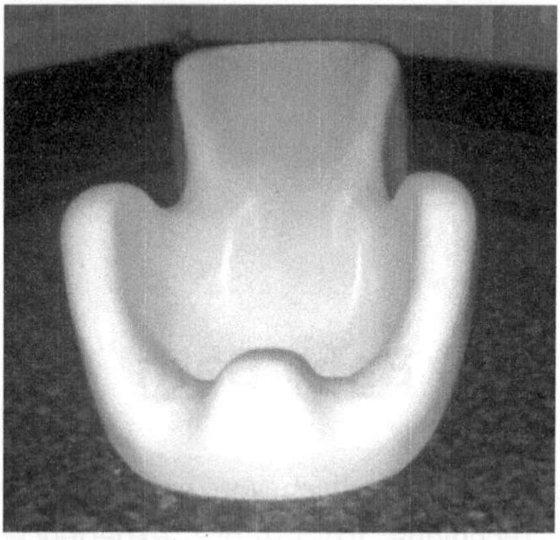

Fig 22: Bath tub

Your ?s My Answers:

How do I bathe my baby?

To bathe your baby, do the following:

1. Undress the baby carefully in a room which is warm enough for her/him. Take the baby to the bath tub. Hold her/him with one arm, taking care to support the head in your palm. The baby should be facing you and the trunk should be at a lower level than the head.

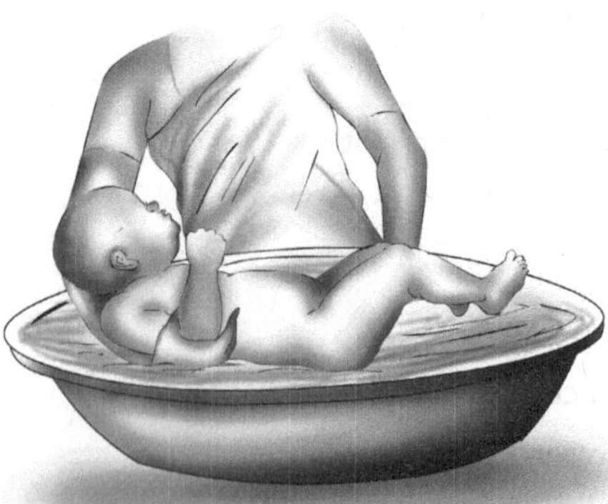

Fig: 23 Method of holding the baby when bathing the baby in the bath tub

2. Wipe the eyes from the inner corner to the outer corner gently with wet cotton balls, using different cotton balls for each eye.

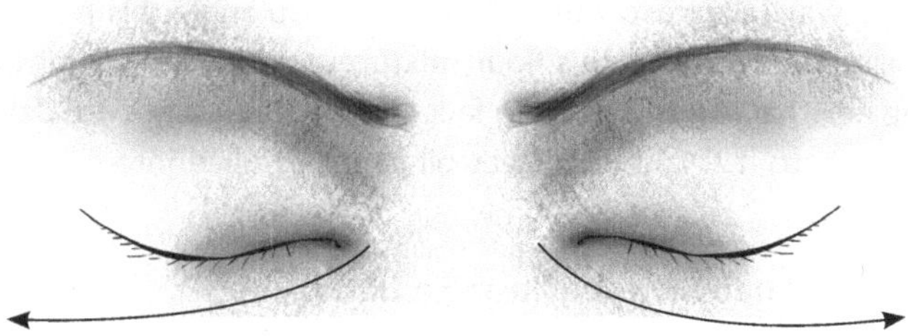

Fig: 24 Direction of cleaning the eyes

3. Soak the cotton cloth in the bowl of warm water; squeeze it out until it is just damp. Wipe the face, neck, head and the area behind the ears. Wipe the hands and feet gently. Apply baby shampoo to the scalp and rinse it off thoroughly using the cotton cloth to squeeze out water onto the scalp in such a way that water doesn't come onto the face or into the ears. Now wipe the trunk, legs and arms. Apply soap on the trunk, legs and arms and rinse it off thoroughly using the damp cotton cloth to squeeze out water on to the body, or by gently splashing water on to the body. Wipe the genital area taking care to clean the stool area the last. Make sure that soap or water does not get into the eyes, ears, mouth, or the nose. Make sure that the water is lukewarm, and not too hot or too cold. Make sure that the bath tub is clean dry and non slippery and has an outlet for the water to drain out. Make sure that the room is at an amicable temperature. Dry your baby using a soft towel. Never carry the baby with wet and slippery hands. Dry the baby immediately after bath and carry him/her in the towel for dressing up.

How often do I need to bathe the scalp of my baby?

Bathing the scalp once or twice a week would suffice. Once the baby becomes one month of age, you can gradually do away with cotton balls, sponges, and wash clothes etc., and start bathing the baby with your hands. Bath tubs which have a good drain and a good head support are the best.

How do I massage my baby? Is it necessary to massage my baby?

Massaging the baby with oil before giving bath is a good practice. You can use olive oil or coconut oil for the massage. Massage should be given in such a way that the baby enjoys it. Be gentle. There is no need to apply the traditional mixture of basin, turmeric and atta for the massage. People do it because it removes the hair on the baby's body. The hair on the newborn's body will anyway fall irrespective of whether you apply this mixture or not for the massage. Neither is this flour mixture going to stop your baby from developing new hair on the body. In fact some babies may even develop skin rash secondary to it. Make sure that oil is not instilled into the eyes, nose, ears and mouth.

Can I bathe my baby without using a bath tub?

The age old Indian practice of keeping babies on the mother's stretched out legs and bathing them is a very convenient one, provided mothers take care to keep the head at a higher level than the trunk. Most mothers do this by keeping their feet on a one foot high stool. Here the gap between the mother's two legs acts as a drain for the water.

❑❑❑

Head

Most of the brain growth occurs in the first 2 years of life; and it is almost complete by the time the child is 4 years of age. Head circumference is measured serially by the paediatricians during the well baby visits; and is charted on the growth chart. Any deviation from the normal needs to be followed up and managed appropriately.

Baby learns to have partial head control by around 3 months of age. He/ she will be able to hold the head completely steady only by around 5 months of age. Till then, utmost care needs to be taken in supporting the baby's head and neck will picking the baby up and while holding the baby upright.

Your ?s My Answers:

My baby is just born. She has some kind of swelling over her head. What is it?

It is due to collection of fluid in the scalp. It is a normal phenomenon. It will disappear in 2 or 3 days. Sometimes, the swelling may persist due to collection of blood under the skin. Such persistent lesions need to be brought to the attention of the paediatrician. A careful follow up is needed.

There are flat depressions over my baby's head. The one at the front is as big as 2-3 cm, and there is one at the back as big as my finger tip of the head. Is it normal?

Yes. Perfectly normal, unless they are too big or too small. These gaps between the skull bones will gradually close as the baby grows. The one at the front should disappear by around 18 months of age (sometimes as early as 9 months) and the one at the back by 6-8 weeks of age. Otherwise it is abnormal, and needs to be evaluated.

My baby tends to put her head on her left side always. I am worried she may develop flattening of her head on that side.

There is nothing much that you can do about it. Try rolling up a towel and placing it in such a way as to restrict movement of her head to the sides when she is sleeping. Such things to restrict the movement of the head are available in shops selling baby products. Even if she develops some flattening, it is going to get corrected as she grows up.

Fig: 25 Pillow designed to restrict the movement of the head of the baby

My baby's head appears to be large? Is it okay?

Generally large babies tend to have a proportionately larger head and vice versa. This larger head size can also be a feature in your family. Unusually large head can point towards some abnormality in the brain. Let a paediatrician examine your child and decide about further management.

❑❑❑

13

Mouth

Generally a newborn doesn't need much of mouth care (mouth care usually starts at around 5-6 months of age). In case the milk forms a thick layer over the tongue, you can gently clean it with a soft, clean and wet cotton cloth (this is very rarely necessary). Sometimes a curd like layer forms in the baby's mouth due to fungal infection. The same infection may be present over the mother's nipples. Consult a doctor in such a case.

Your ?s My Answers:

My baby is 3 weeks of age. There is a boil on his upper lip in the centre. My doctor asked me not to bother about it. Is it okay?

Yes. It is called 'sucking blister'. It is going to disappear in due course. It is not going to cause any discomfort to your baby.

There are whitish pearl like lesions on the roof of my baby's mouth. What are they?

They are called 'epsteins pearls'. They will disappear in a few weeks. Similar lesions can also be found on the gums some times.

My baby has a cleft in the roof of his mouth. How do I feed him? What do I do for it?

Firstly talk to the paediatrician and clarify all your doubts. It is better that you talk to him/her about the various ways to feed your baby. This cleft needs to be operated before your baby is one year of age; otherwise his speech development will be affected.

My baby has a split in his upper lip from birth. Will it interfere with his speech development?

No. Now it is more important to address the problem of feeding. You can discuss with the paediatrician about it. He is likely to be operated before he is 3 months of age. He may need revision surgeries later on also.

My baby has 2 teeth on the lower gum from birth. Should I get them removed?

They may be prematurely erupted milk teeth or they may be extra teeth.. Let the dentist decide about their extraction. Do not worry about them as long as they are not causing any problem to you or the baby.

My baby is 1 month of age. Recently one tooth erupted on the lower jaw. Should I get it removed?

Talk to your dentist. Look at the previous query.

❑❑❑

14

Nose and Ears

There are certain issues regarding nose and ears that worry many mothers. I tried to answer most queries related to these issues in the following pages

Your ?s My Answers:

My baby is 2 weeks of age. His nose gets stuffy sometimes. He finds it difficult to breathe at such times; and becomes very irritable. What can I do?

This is a common problem with babies. Keep Normal Saline nasal drops at home always. Do not bother as long as the nose runs a little bit, but is not stuffy. Instill two drops in each nostril whenever the nose is stuffy. Keep the baby on your lap in such a way that his head is slightly lower than the rest of the body while instilling the drops; otherwise he may aspirate. Do not instill the drops immediately after feeds. Sometimes stuffy nose can also result in ear pain because the secretions from the nose block a tube which connects the ear to the nose. The baby will become very irritable at such times. If your baby has fever or cough, if he breathes too fast, or if he is too irritable, get a paediatrician's opinion. Ask your paediatrician to demonstrate to you at least once the position in which your baby has to be held for instilling the drops.

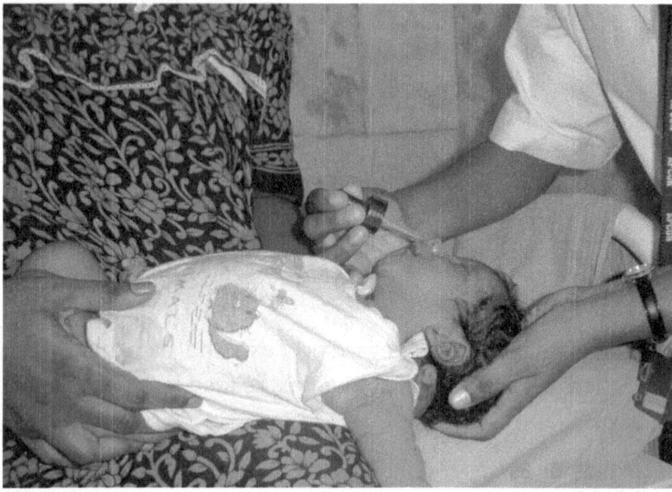

Fig: 26 Instilling nasal drops

My baby sneezes quite often. Should I give her some medicine?

No. Sneezing is quite common among newborns. Nothing needs to be done unless she develops running nose, nasal stuffiness, cough or fever.

My baby is 4 weeks of age and her breathing is noisy. What is the problem likely to be?

Your baby's nose might be stuffy. You can relieve her of her discomfort by instilling nasal drops. If her breathing had been noisy since birth, do consult a paediatrician. Your baby might be suffering from weakness of her airway, which generally gets resolved over a time. Paediatrician's opinion is a must. If your baby appears sick, has fever, cough etc or appears very uncomfortable, get a paediatrician's opinion immediately. Keep the house dust and dander free to prevent allergies and infections of the airways and lungs.

My newborn baby has protruding ears. What can I do about them?

His ears need to be bandaged in such a way that they remain flat; otherwise he may face a lot of embarrassment when he grows older. Meet your doctor immediately and discuss about the problem.

My newborn baby has some skin tag in front of his ear. Is it okay?

Most of the times, an ear tag can be ignored unless it is causing a cosmetic problem. Sometimes, these ear tags may be associated with abnormalities of the kidney and hearing defects. A thorough evaluation by a paediatrician and an ENT specialist is a must. Once associated abnormalities are ruled out, ear tags can be surgically removed for cosmetic reasons.

My new born daughter has a pit in front of her ear. Is it normal?

Ear pits , generally, are not problematic. Rarely, they may be associated with other abnormalities of the face, hearing defects and abnormalities of the kidney. A thorough evaluation by a paediatrician and an ENT specialist is a must. The ear pits require surgical removal if they are getting infected often.

When can I get my daughter's ears pierced?

You can get your daughter's ears pierced as early as 1 month of age. The pain will be less and the process will be easier if it is done early. It is better to get it done from a clinic where they use the 'gun' technique to pierce the baby's ears. The technique is completely sterile. It is safer and less painful than the conventional one. There is one problem with getting the ears pierced early. The holes may start looking asymmetrical as the child grows. In such a case you may have to get the ears pierced again.

My son is 6 months of age. I feel he doesn't respond to sound. He doesn't turn around when I call him. Is it okay?

No. you should meet a paediatrician and an ENT specialist immediately. Complete assessment of his hearing needs to be done. Any rectifiable defect with his ear needs to be rectified as early as possible. Generally brain growth is almost complete by 4 years of age. Most of the language is also learnt in these 4 years of age. Hearing is absolutely necessary for your child to develop language function. So, do not delay. Meet the doctor immediately.

❑❑❑

15

Eyes

Babies can see right from the time they are born. They close their eyes to bright light. They start fixing their eyes on the mother's face by around one to one and half months; after which they start smiling at her. New borns cannot coordinate both the eyes to form a single image. They will be able to coordinate both the eyes by around 4 months of age. Any squint (crossed eyes) persisting after this age needs a thorough evaluation by an eye specialist. Newborn babies do not produce tears when the cry. It generally takes around a month or two for babies to produce tears while crying.

Your ?s My Answers:

My baby is 3 weeks of age. There is persistent watery discharge from his eyes for the past 2 days. What should I do?

Most babies do not produce tears till around 3 weeks of age. Some may produce tears as early as five days. These tears drain into the nose via a tube connecting the eyes and the nose. Many babies have a block in this tube which usually resolves by one year of age. Your baby might also be having such a block. Massaging this tube several times a day by firm pressure will help. Get a paediatrician's opinion and learn the technique of massaging the tube. The doctors may decide to operate to remove the block if the problem doesn't get resolved by 1 year of age.

My baby is one week of age. He appears to have 'crossed eyes' (eyes appear to turn inward). What should I do?

It is a common complaint by many mothers. A newborn baby's eyes will take time to mature and develop correct alignment. The eyes will become straight by around 4 months of age. Moreover the skin covering the inner part of the eye also tends to make it look as if the baby has 'crossed eyes'.

Get a paediatrician's opinion once to make sure that there is no squint, or any other eye problem.

My baby is 2 weeks of age. She does not have tears in her eyes when she cries. Is it normal?

Yes. New born babies do not produce tears in the first few weeks.

My new born baby has something whitish on her pupil. Is it normal?

No. Meet a paediatrician/ophthalmologist (eye doctor) immediately. It can be something affecting the inner as well as the outer parts of the eye and will require thorough evaluation and treatment.

My baby was born in the 7th month. Doctor advised me to get her eyes checked periodically. Is it necessary?

Yes. It is very important for you to follow your doctor's instructions strictly. Premature babies have a tendency to develop certain problems with their eyes which can even result in blindness if proper treatment is not given to prevent them.

My daughter, 4 months of age, developed redness of one eye and yellowish discharge from that eye. My neighbour told me that she might be having 'conjunctivitis'. Can babies develop conjunctivitis?

Yes. Conjunctivitis of eye is most commonly due to some infection or allergy. Your baby seems to have developed conjunctivitis due to some infection. Consult an ophthalmologist (eye doctor) immediately.

❑❑❑

16

Umbilicus (Belly Button)

The umbilical cord is either clamped or tied with a sterile thread in the hospital. The cord is cleaned from base upwards using gauze soaked in 1% isopropyl alcohol/spirit twice a day, or 1% gentian violet is applied to it to keep it from getting infected. The cord usually falls off between 5 to 9 days. If it doesn't, do consult a doctor. You can clean the cord while bathing the baby. You can wash it with soap and water. Sponge bath is preferred till the umbilical cord falls off. Pat it dry after bath. Do not unnecessarily handle the cord, or touch the raw area once the cord has fallen off. Do not try to pull it off. Allow it to fall by itself. Ensure that stool matter does not come in contact with the cord. Ensure that the diaper worn by the baby does not come in contact with the cord. If there is any discharge from the umbilical area, or if the surrounding area looks red and swollen, consult a doctor urgently because umbilical infection is a serious infection. It needs to be treated immediately.

Your ?s My Answers:

My baby has a big umbilicus protruding from the tummy. Is it okay?

Many babies have what your baby is having. It is called 'umbilical hernia'. It usually resolves by 1 year of age. A surgery may be needed if it is too big, or if it persists beyond 1 or 2 years of age. Thyroid problems should be ruled out. Get your paediatrician's opinion once.

My baby is having watery discharge from her umbilicus and there is a pinkish swelling in the umbilical area. Will it heal?

It is something called 'umbilical granuloma'. If it is very small, it may resolve with good umblical care. It may need to be treated by the paediatrician with few applications of certain chemicals. Do get your paediatrician's opinion. Infection and other problems need to be ruled out.

❑❑❑

17

Breasts and Genitalia

There are certain issues about breasts and genitalia of the baby that confuse many parents. Their queries can range from the size of breasts, discharge from vagina to tight fore skin and absent testis. Certain common queries have been answered in the following pages.

Your ?s My Answers:

My baby is 3 days of age. He has swollen breasts. I am worried.

Swelling of breasts in the newborn period is due to the mother's hormones which enter the baby's blood. The swelling will disappear in 2-4 weeks time. Do not press or squeeze the breasts; otherwise you may cause them to get infected. Some times even milk will be discharged from the breast for a few days. Do not worry about it. Consult your paediatrician if the breasts appear red, excessively swollen, or if they become tender.

My baby is one week of age. She is having a white coloured discharge from her vagina since 4 days . Why?

There can be discharge from the vagina at 2 to 3 days of life. It can persist up to 2 weeks. Some times there can be blood stained discharge from the vagina at the end of 1st week of life due to withdrawal of mother's hormones from the baby's blood. This type of discharge should not persist for more than 2-3 days. Anyway better get a paediatrician's opinion once.

My baby has testis only on one side. The testis bag on the other side is empty. What should I do?

Let the paediatrician advise you regarding the future course especially if the testis bag still remains empty at 6 months of age. Do not neglect the problem. Careful follow up with the paediatrician is a must. The problem needs to be rectified before the child is 15 months of age.

Some times stimulation of the inner side of the upper thigh will cause the testis to move up into the abdomen. This is called 'retractile testis'. Your baby's paediatrician will be able to differentiate this condition from the previous one. Nothing needs to be done for this condition(retractile testis).

❑❑❑

18

Travel

It is better to avoid travel with newborns; but in case it is unavoidable take some precautions so that your travel with the baby doesn't become a torrid experience. Do not travel in overcrowded vehicles. Dress the baby adequately as explained in the previous sections. Carry adequate food and drinking water for yourself. Continue breast feeding whenever the baby cries for feeds. In case you are uncomfortable with the idea of feeding the baby in the public, carry expressed breast milk and spoons. Take care to keep the milk cool so that it stays for at least 4 hours without getting spoilt.

Your ?s My Answers:

What should I carry with me while travelling with my baby?

You must carry the following items with you while travelling with your baby:

Normal Saline nasal drops:

If the baby develops nasal stuffiness, and finds it difficult to breathe; instill one or two drops in each nostril taking care to hold the baby's head a bit lower than body.

Good quality diapers:

The diapers should be made of absorbent gelling materials (AGMs) and be non-medicated, soft, fit snugly, and keep the baby dry.

Syrup paracetamol (or drops):

Ask your paediatrician for the dose before you embark upon your travel; and administer it to the baby accordingly if the baby develops fever. Get a paediatrician's opinion as soon as possible. Always make sure you have the paediatrician's phone number with you.

Clean and soft cotton (or non-medicated baby wipes):

For cleaning the baby when he/she passes stools/urine.

Soap/Hand sanitiser:

To keep your hands clean so that the baby doesn't catch any infection.

ORS (Oral Rehydration Solution) packets:

These are available in all medical shops. Buy WHO recommended formulations only. If the baby develops diarrhoea; increase breast feeds and intermittently give ORS (using spoon), in addition to the breast milk.

Follow the simple instructions given on the ORS sachet for preparing the rehydration solution. Always use sterile drinking water for preparing the solution. Continue this process of giving breast feeds, ORS till you can consult a doctor.

Disposal bag:

For disposing the wipes, diapers etc.

You should also carry *extra clothes, towels* etc.

Boiled water:

Boil water for 10 minutes after the bubbles appear. Cool it and carry it in a clean and sterilised bottle (bottle boiled in water for 10 minutes after the water starts boiling). You may need this water for preparing ORS, for cleaning the baby etc.

Why do I have to feed my baby during take off and landing in case of a flight journey?

Always feed the baby during take off and landing in case of air travel because the process of suckling will make sure that the baby doesn't develop ear block (something like how chewing helps us from developing ear pain during air travel).

All said and done it is better to avoid travelling with the baby unless absolutely necessary.

❑❑❑

Vaccination and Prevention of Infection

It is very important for the parents to know why we vaccinate kids. Vaccines stimulate the immune system of the child to produce substances to fight specific infections for which the vaccines are intended for. These infections can endanger the life of the child, can cause permanent sequelae like paralysis and various other complications. Therefore it is imperative that your child be vaccinated against these infections.

Baby should receive BCG, OPV before discharge from hospital. Hepatitis B can be given either before discharge from hospital, or at 6 weeks depending on the hospital policy and the subsequent doses can be given depending on when the first dose was given. Get your baby's complete immunisation schedule before discharge from hospital. Here is the vaccination schedule being followed in India:

At Birth	BCG, OPV 0, Hepatitis B 1
6 weeks (1 ½ months)	OPV 1, DPT 1, Hepatitis B 2
10 weeks (2 ½ months)	OPV 2, DPT 2
14 weeks (3 ½ months)	OPV 3, DPT 3
6 months	Hepatitis B 3
9 months	Measles
15 months	MMR
18 months	OPV booster 1, DPT booster 1
2 years	Typhoid
5 years	OPV booster 2, DPT booster 2, Typhoid
8 years and every 3 years	Typhoid
10 years and every 5 years	TT booster

Some important points:

1. Haemophilus influenzae B vaccine (HiB) which protects the baby from meningitis caused by Haemophilus influenzae B is a very important vaccine; and should be incorporated into the immunisation schedule. Ask your paediatrician about it and make sure that your baby receives HiB as per the schedule.

2. Hepatitis A, Chicken Pox, Flu, Rota virus and Pneumococcal vaccines are optional vaccines dT should be preferred to TT if available

Some precautions to be taken after vaccination:

- Do not rub the area of vaccination.
- Do not apply anything there at the site of vaccination.
- Do not give any thing hot to eat or drink for 1 hour after administering Polio drops (breast feeds can be given).

Given below are certain complications which may occur in some cases:

- **Minor reactions** like fever, swelling and redness at vaccine site, pain etc is common after vaccination. Giving the child Paracetamol syrup for one day as per your paediatrician's advice will take care of most of these problems.
- **Severe reactions** like 'fits' and 'shock' are extremely rare; but in case your child had a severe reaction during any of the vaccinations inform the doctor about it during the subsequent vaccinations so that that particular vaccine which caused the reaction can be avoided (otherwise the vaccination may prove fatal to your child).

Some more information about vaccination:

- DaPT causes less pain and fever than DPT, but is more expensive. The chance of serious reactions is less with DaPT. I suggest that you give DaPT to the baby instead of DPT if you can afford it.
- Injectable polio vaccine is also available and gives better protection to the child than oral polio vaccine. However, it is very expensive. In India we still prefer to give oral polio drops because it is believed that they give better protection against acquiring infection via drinking water and food. It is advised that you give OPV also to your child along with Injectable polio vaccine in case you are able to afford the injectable polio vaccine. Pulse polio programmes are organised to vaccinate all

the children at the same time, and spread the vaccine strain of the virus in the community so that we eradicate polio from our country. I suggest you give polio drops to your child during all the pulse polio programmes irrespective of his /her regular vaccination schedule.

- Nowadays combination preparations are available for various vaccines to save the baby the trouble of being poked too many times. You can find more about them from your paediatrician.
- Some vaccines like chicken pox and measles can either be given together on the same day at different sites; or be given at least 1 month apart.

This section, though, is written to explain to the mothers the art of caring for babies up to 6 months of age; I gave a brief idea about the complete vaccination schedule here as I feel that mothers should be aware of it from the very beginning.

Your ?s My Answers:

Can you tell me something more about the diseases against which I am going to vaccinate my baby?

I will give a brief idea about each disease against which you need to vaccinate your child.

BCG is given to protect the child against **TB (tuberculosis).** A scar will form at the site of vaccination by the time the baby is around 3 months of age. Tuberculosis can affect any part of the body including lungs and brain; and in its most severe form can even result in death.

OPV (oral polio drops) are given to protect the child against **polio** which can cause paralysis of limbs and some times it can also affect the brain and rarely even result in death.

DPT is given to protect the child against 3 dreaded diseases namely **diphtheria** (black cough), **pertussis**(whooping cough) and **Tetanus**(which causes rigidity and spasm of limbs and jaws). These diseases can even result in the death of the child.

Hepatitis B vaccine protects your child against a type of jaundice which spreads via blood, by sharing needles, by sexual intercourse and from mother to baby. This type of jaundice can some times prove fatal.

Hib protects your baby against a type of brain fever (meningitis to be precise) caused by Haemophilus influenza B in addition to protecting the baby against pneumonia (lung infection), sepsis (blood infection) etc caused by the same.

Measles vaccine protects your baby against measles which causes fever, rash, pneumonia (lung infection) and sometimes even brain infection.

MMR protects the baby against **measles, mumps** (swelling of those glands behind the jaws) and **rubella** (causes fever with rash). Mumps can some times result in boys becoming infertile, can affect other systems of the body, and cause serious complications. Rubella can cause defects in the baby while in the womb if mother develops rubella during pregnancy.

Typhoid vaccine protects the child against **typhoid fever** which can affect many systems of the body. It has to be repeated every 3 years for better efficacy.

Hepatitis A protects the child against a type of jaundice which spreads via food and water and which can rarely prove to be fatal.

Chicken pox vaccine, as the name implies, protects the child against **chicken pox** (the child develops fever and boils all over the body). Chicken pox also can sometimes lead to pneumonia and brain fever.

Pneumococcal vaccine protects the child against infections caused by pneumococcus which range from pneumonia to brain fever (meningitis to be precise).

Of late, vaccine to prevent cervical cancer i.e. cancer of the lower part of the womb is also available. This is given to girls after 10 to 12 years of age.

Vaccines to prevent certain types of brain fever, rabies (due to the bite of dogs and certain other animals), and flu are available. They are given only in special circumstances, as like when the child is at high risk to develop these infections. Talk to your paediatrician about them.

Can you tell me something about vaccine storage?

Vaccines lose their strength if not stored properly. Ensure that the hospital has generator backed cold storage (fridge/ vaccine storage box) for the vaccines. In case you buy them from a medical shop, ensure the same. Some vaccines should not be frozen, and some need to be stored in the freezer. Be aware of this fact and read the instructions on the label before storing them temporarily in your fridge. It is preferable that you get your child vaccinated in a hospital which keeps the vaccines in the hospital itself. In case you need to carry the vaccines from the medical shop to the nursing home, ensure that cold temperature is maintained while carrying them. Some medical shops provide you with a box filled with frozen ice. Let the vaccine vials not come in direct contact with the ice or ice box. Keep them in a polythene bag; and then keep that polythene bag in another polythene bag containing ice/ ice box. OPV vial has a lavender coloured square on its label. If this square becomes dark, it implies that the vaccine has not been stored properly and has lost its potency.

Fig: 27 The 3 OPV vials on the right contain OPV which has lost its potency (the squares have turned dark)

How effective are these vaccines?

Most of them are very effective (almost 95%) if stored properly and administered properly.

What should I do if I miss any of the scheduled vaccinations for my baby? Do I have to repeat the whole cycle?

You do not have to repeat the whole cycle. Just start from the dose you missed and go ahead. Get a new schedule written by your paediatrician; starting from the missed dose.

Can I give my baby her scheduled vaccination when she has cough and cold?

There is absolutely no problem with that. Mild fever, cough, cold, diarrhoea etc need not stop you from vaccinating your daughter. In case the child is having severe diarrhoea, you can postpone those vaccines which are given by mouth. There are some contraindications like serious reactions to previous dose of the same vaccine, immunosuppressed states etc for vaccinating a child. You can know more about them by talking to your paediatrician.

My baby was born in the 8th month of my pregnancy. Does her vaccination schedule differ from that of other babies?

No. She will have the same schedule as the other babies. There may be a need for delaying the first dose of hepatitis B vaccine in babies weighing less than 2 kgs as adequate immunity may not be conferred by giving the vaccine to babies weighing less than 2 kgs. One can wait till the baby picks up some weight. It is better to discuss about this issue with your paediatrician.

My baby boy did not develop a scar after BCG vaccination. Do I need to repeat it?

Yes. You need to repeat it before he is 1 year of age. Ensure that BCG and measles vaccination are not given on the same day. There should be a gap of at least 1 month between BCG vaccination and measles vaccination.

Any other precaution that I should take while getting my son vaccinated?

Ensure the usage of disposable syringes and needles.

How do I protect my baby from infection?

To protect your baby from infections follow the instructions given below:

- Avoid keeping the baby in overcrowded rooms.
- Do not let the baby be handled by those with cough, cold, fever etc.
- Do not let anybody smoke near the baby.
- Keep your hands clean always. Use disinfectant soap for hand washing.
- Do not let too many people handle the baby, especially if you cannot make sure that they wash their hands before handling the baby.
- If you notice any boils over your nipples, consult a doctor immediately and take his/her advice regarding your treatment and regarding feeding the baby.
- In case you yourself are suffering from cough, cold fever etc; at least take care not to sneeze or cough over the baby's face.
- If you have boils in your nose or anywhere else, consult your doctor and get treated. Always wash your hands before touching the baby with the same hands with which you handled the boils.
- Good umbilical (belly button) care is important, but do not touch the umbilical area unnecessarily.When the baby passes stools and you

clean the genital area; avoid soiling of other parts of the genital area with stool matter so as to prevent infection of her urine.

- Vaccinating your child against dangerous infections is very important.
- Protect the child from mosquitoes to prevent dangerous infections like malaria and dengue.

When should I consult a doctor? I mean when should I suspect that my baby might be sick?

Suspect that your baby might be sick in the following circumstances:

- If your baby is sleeping more than usual
- If your baby has fever
- If your baby has cough and cold
- If your baby is crying inconsolably irrespective of whatever you do to console the baby
- If your baby is not feeding well
- If your baby is breathing faster than usual, making unusual sounds while breathing, and appears uncomfortable while breathing
- If your baby appears sick, is not active, appears bluish or very pale, and is very cold to feel
- If your baby has vomiting and diarrhoea
- If your baby has not passed urine for more than 12 hours
- If your baby has not passed stools for 4 or more days, or is passing red or black stools
- If there is a persistent swelling over the head

I have not mentioned some serious conditions like seizures (fits) here because you are going to take the baby to the hospital anyway in such a situation. Here I would like to say some thing about 'fits' (seizures). Seizures occur due to changes in the electrical activity of the brain and result in sudden onset of abnormal rhythmic body movements, changes in behavior and loss of consciousness. The baby may just stop responding to you. In any case, fits can endanger life and can also point towards some underlying serious condition. Children can choke during an episode of seizures. In the chapter on 'first aid and emergencies', I have given a brief idea about what needs to be done in such situations

❑❑❑

20

Prevention of Accidents

Prevention of accidents is a very important aspect of baby care. The children in the age group 0-6 months have restricted movement; therefore most of the dangers/accidents are caused to them due to the negligence or carelessness of the parent. We must know that most accidents are due to fall from the bed, hot liquids falling on the baby, accidental suffocation, bath related and temperature related. By applying our wisdom, and common sense, we can avoid many tragic and potential mishaps

Following tips will guide you to some extent about how to prevent accidents from happening:

- **Do not leave the baby unattended when on the bed**, especially once he/she learns to roll over. Always lock the wheels of the crib and pram if you are going to leave the baby alone even for a moment. Always use the belt when the baby is in the pram.
- **Do not leave burning objects and warmers in the room when the baby is sleeping.**
- **Let the mattress be not too soft**, otherwise the baby may accidentally suffocate. Similarly, do not have soft pillows and toys on the bed when the baby is sleeping. The baby should either be put in the crib for sleeping, or next to the mother provided the bed is spacious and precautions have been taken to ensure that the baby doesn't roll over and fall down. Ropes and wires should not be present in the baby crib, otherwise accidental strangulation can happen.
- Keep the baby adequately clothed in winters.
- **Never attempt to make the baby swallow tablets.** Always hold the baby in your lap in semi-sitting position while giving tonics, fluids or food; otherwise she/he may aspirate. Have a look at the following pages for a better idea.

- Do not handle the baby when you have hot objects or sharp objects in your hand.
- Do not apply cosmetic products on the baby including kajal to her eyes.
- Do not leave the baby in the care of a young child.
- When you are giving bath to the baby, make sure that the tub is not slippery. **Make sure the water is lukewarm; and not too hot or cold**. Never leave the baby alone in the bath even for a second.
- **Administer medicines accurately** as prescribed by the doctor
- **Do not drink anything hot while holding the baby.**
- **Do not leave the baby unattended in the bath tub.**

❑❑❑

21

Miscellaneous

Some miscellaneous queries have been answered in this chapter. I hope I have answered most of the common questions posed by mothers about their babies upto 6 months of age.

Your ?s My Answers:

My baby is one week of age. Whenever I hold her close to me, I can feel her heart beat. It beats very fast. Is it normal?

Yes. The heart of a baby beats much faster than that of an adult. Do not worry if your baby is fine otherwise.

Can you tell me something about babies who are born with a hole in the heart?

A normal heart has 4 chambers. There can be a hole in the wall separating the 2 upper chambers (atria) or the 2 lower chambers (ventricles). There can also be abnormal communications between major blood vessels which carry blood from the body to the heart and from the heart to the lungs. There can also be a combination of various such defects in the heart. Depending on the type of defect and the location of defect the baby can be born blue, can be born with a failing heart or can be born without any problem at birth. Even if the baby appears completely normal at birth, he/ she may develop failure of heart or may start becoming blue at a later age. This blueness is due to mixing of pure and impure blood. Growth of the baby will be affected and life threatening complications can occur later on. Good medical and surgical treatment options are available for treating these defects at an appropriate age (mostly before one year of age). These can be discussed with the paediatrician on an individual basis. Some holes and communications may close all by themselves as the baby grows up and may not cause any further problem. This aspect too can be discussed with the paediatrician on an individual basis.

Can you tell me something about the long-term problems with preterm babies?

By definition, preterm babies are babies born more than three weeks before the due date. The more prematurely a baby is born, the more likely is the chance of the baby having both short-term and long-term problems. The baby may have problems with breathing, maintaining temperature and feeding. The more premature a baby is the more the risk of aspiration during feeds. Premature babies are more prone to infections. They can develop many serious complications related to lungs, heart, brain, gut etc in the new born period. Generally, babies born in the 9th month and those who have not remained in the new born intensive care unit for prolonged periods do not have any major long-term problems.

Very premature babies who were in the hospital for prolonged periods due to various complications and those who have received oxygen and other forms of treatment for long periods will tend to have long-term problems like behavioural problems, poor IQ, hearing impairment, spasticity (muscles of the body will be tight and weak in these babies), fits, chronic lung problems, poor physical and mental growth, squint, poor vision, damage to the retina of the eye causing loss of vision etc.

It is a must that these babies are followed up and examined by the paediatrician regularly so that the problems can be identified and necessary treatment be given at the earliest. Parents need to strictly follow the paediatrician's guidelines regarding these follow up visits.

My baby is 4 days of age. She developed jaundice on the 2nd day after birth. The paediatrician told me not to worry about it. Is it okay?

Your baby is having something called 'physiological jaundice'. It occurs in many babies. Nothing needs to be done unless the jaundice appears severe, or stays for longer than 10 days (normally it should disappear in 5-7 days). Getting your paediatrician's opinion for the second time is important so that severe jaundice is not missed. The paediatrician may order a blood test in case it is severe, and accordingly advise you. Severe jaundice can harm your baby's brain, and so do not ignore it even if you have the slightest doubt.

Here I would like to tell mothers with preterm babies (babies born much before the expected date of delivery) that this kind of jaundice in preterms can stay up to 7-10 days. If it persists beyond 14 days, then it is not physiological anymore and needs complete evaluation. Any jaundice appearing on the first day of life (up to 36 hours of life), persisting beyond 10 days of life (14 days in preterms), appearing after 14 days of life, appearing severe, or appearing to be associated with the passage of chalky white stools needs thorough evaluation.

What injections should my baby receive at birth?

Vitamin K injection is given immediately after birth. Later on the bacteria present in your baby's gut will take over and start synthesising Vitamin K for the body. BCG vaccine needs to be given before discharge from hospital. This vaccine is for protecting your child against tuberculosis. The first dose of Hepatitis B vaccine can also be given before discharge from hospital, though it can be given at a later date unless the mother is positive for Hepatitis B surface antigen. If the mother is positive for Hepatitis B surface antigen, the vaccine has to be given within 12 hours of birth and the respective immunoglobulin too needs to be given at the earliest at a different site (though it is said that the immunoglobulin can be given up to 7 days of age).

My blood group is A negative and my husband's is A positive. My baby's blood group is A positive. The doctor gave me an injection called 'anti D' immediately after my baby was born.Why?

Whenever the mother's blood group is negative, father's positive and the baby's positive; mother's blood prepares substances which can destroy the next baby's blood cells. These substances are more likely to destroy the blood cells of the next baby if his/her blood group is also positive. This destruction of blood cells can cause severe anaemia (thinning of blood), jaundice and sometimes death of the next baby. Anti D is an injection given to prevent this from happening so that your next baby doesn't develop anaemia and jaundice due to the destruction of blood cells even if the blood group is positive. All pregnant mothers whose blood group is negative with their husband's being positive should carefully follow up with their obstetrician.

The problem of anaemia and jaundice can occur even when mother has O blood group and the baby has A, B, or AB blood groups. This will be managed appropriately by the paediatrician, and there is no injection to prevent this.

My baby's left foot is always turned inwards. Should I show it to a doctor?

Yes. She might be having club foot. A paediatrician's opinion is a must. Other bone and spine problems need to be ruled out. It has to be treated early so that the deformity does not become permanent.

I hear a click in the left hip of my baby boy some times. What should I do about it?

Some times such clicks can be heard normally; but some times the click may be due to some problem in the hip joint. Do not ignore them. Otherwise your son may end up being lame when he grows up. Get your paediatrician to assess the baby as soon as possible.

Can I clip my baby's nails?

Yes. You should do it carefully. Baby nail clippers are available in the market. Nail clipping should preferably be done when the baby is sleeping.

How do I protect my baby from mosquitoes?

Using mosquito net is the safest way of protecting babies from mosquitoes, especially when the babies still have not acquired the ability to move from wherever they have been put to sleep. Mosquito nets specially designed for babies are available in the market. Wire mesh to the doors and windows is also an effective method to ward off mosquitoes. Clothe the baby adequately. Do not use mosquito repellants on the body; as they can cause allergy and also toxic reactions when they get absorbed through the skin. It is preferable not to use mosquito coils, mats and liquid vaporisers etc as they can cause allergies and breathing problems. Do not apply essential oils like eucalyptus oil to the baby's skin as they can cause allergic reactions. Avoid all these chemicals and plant products as much as possible; especially during the first 6 months (preferably for the first 3 years of life) at least. If you still want to use liquid vaporisers, you can switch them on for 2-3 hours during which time the baby should not be in the room. You can bring the baby into the room some time after switching them off. Applying coconut oil to the exposed parts, and keeping essential oils like eucalyptus oil or neem oil soaked cloth somewhere in the room (not very close to the baby) is our very own 'grand mother's method of effectively driving away the mosquitoes. Keep the house and surroundings clean and dry so as to prevent the breeding of mosquitoes.

My baby is 3 months of age. He sucks at his thumb some times. I am worried that this habit may affect the development of his teeth later on. Is it so?

Almost all babies suck at their fingers some time or the other. This is a natural phenomenon. They may be doing it either because they are hungry, or to comfort themselves, or to satisfy their urge to suck, or to feel secure, or just to explore their body. The onset is usually between 3 and 6 months. It occurs less often in breast fed babies because the urge to suck gets satisfied by suckling at the mother's breast. As long as you spend adequate time with your baby, breast feed your baby properly, and the family environment is good; you don't have to worry about his thumb sucking. He will outgrow it. Thumb sucking will affect the development of teeth only if the habit persists till after 6 years of age when permanent teeth start erupting.

I have a baby 5 months of age. How can I keep an eye on her, and at the same time continue with my daily chores?

You can buy a baby sling with a good head support. You can put your baby in the sling and attach the sling to your body. Good baby slings which enable you to carry your baby on your chest, on your back, and at your sides are available. Some slings are designed in such a way that they enable you to even breast feed your baby while you carry her in the sling. Both your hands will be free now so that you can go ahead with your daily chores. Do not carry the baby into the kitchen when you are cooking something, cutting onions etc using spices, or mixing powdery substances like 'atta' etc.

You can also try using a pram; always making sure that the belt is in place. You can also keep your baby in her crib and check upon her periodically.

My new born baby appears jittery some times. I mean it appears as if she is trembling. Is it normal?

Trembling some times is a normal phenomenon in new born period. Do not bother if her cry, colour and activity are good.

I have given birth to twins. Does their care differ from that of other babies?

Are they born prematurely? If so, take extra care regarding keeping them warm. Breast feed them one after the other; or at the same time depending on your convenience. Their care is no different from other babies except that you have to take more stress to handle two babies at the same time.

What are stem cells? Why did my obstetrician suggest that I save my baby's umbilical cord blood cells for future use?

Stem cells in the umbilical cord blood are cells which can differentiate into various types of blood cells. In case a need arises in the future wherein your child or somebody in the family needs stem cells to treat certain blood cancers and certain other conditions requiring stem cells, these cells which have been preserved can be used for the same purpose. It is easier this way than looking for a donor of stem cells from some other family because it is easier to match the donor stem cells with the recipient's if both belong to the same family.

How do I administer medicines to my baby?

You can give syrups using a spoon. Hold the baby in such a way that your one hand supports the head and neck, and you use the other hand to administer the medicine. Head end should always be at a higher level than the foot end (semi sitting position). ***Never try to administer tablets or capsules.*** Most medicines are available in syrup form. In case a need arises that you have to administer a medicine which is in tablet form, crush it and mix it with a few drops of breast milk, and put it in the baby's mouth using a spoon.

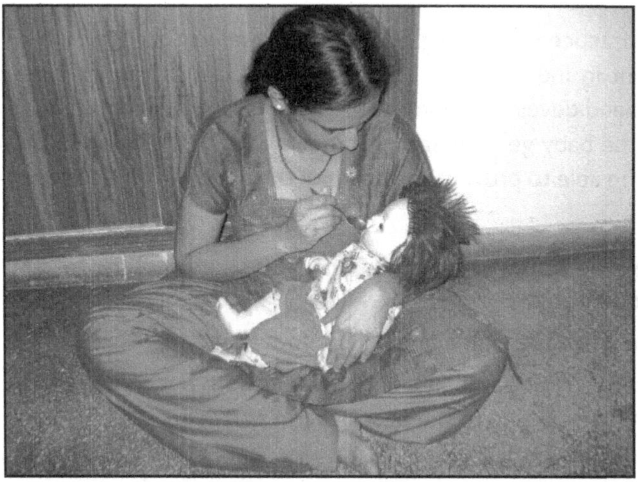

Fig: 28 Technique of holding the baby for administration of medicine

Why should sugar water, gripe water and steroid drops not be given to the baby?

Giving sugar water prior to establishing lactation will delay the establishment of successful breast feeding. Giving sugar water to the baby can increase or prolong baby's jaundice, and also can cause diarrhoea. Some people still talk about giving sugar water to the babies. Kindly do not follow this practice of giving sugar water to the baby. Gripe water contains alcohol and is used by many and advocated by some as a remedy for 'colic'. Studies have shown it not to be effective for treating 'colic', and in fact it may cause diarrhoea. Moreover why would any mother want to give something containing alcohol to her baby? Steroid drops are being sold over the counter in many medical shops. They are commonly bought by mothers over the counter when the baby has cold and fever. They continue to use them without doctor's advice. The baby initially appears well and starts to become chubby. The mother wrongly feels that her baby is looking chubbier and healthier than other babies. These steroid babies are more prone to develop serious infections and high blood pressure etc. Many babies die when they develop these infections because steroids lower the immunity; i.e. the ability to fight infections. So mothers should not buy steroid drops by themselves from the chemist without a doctor's prescription.

Why shouldn't oil be instilled into the nose, mouth and ears of the baby?

This practice of instilling oil into the nose, ears and mouth of the baby is rampant in Indian villages. This leads to the baby aspirating the oil into the lungs and developing something called 'oil instillation pneumonia'; i.e the lungs of the baby get damaged . Sometimes it is so difficult to treat that we may not be able to prevent the death of the baby. Never ever encourage this practice.

Finally, some important points that you should follow for the well being of your baby:

- Exclusive breast feeding is very important.
- Preterm babies need additional nutrition, but this has to be given to them according to the paediatrician's advice.
- In case you are not able to breast feed for some time, use spoon, and not bottle to feed your baby with the expressed milk.
- Do not buy gripe water, steroid drops, multivitamin tonics etc. on your own from the medical shop. These may sometimes prove to be harmful to your baby.
- Do not instill oil into the eyes, ears, nose and mouth.
- Do not blow into the nose.

- Take care that water doesn't go into the nose, eyes, and ears and mouth while bathing the baby. Support the baby's head while bathing her/him. Use only low alkaline soap. Avoid applying soap and powder on the face.
- Do not put the baby to sleep on his/her tummy.
- Clothe the baby adequately and ensure warmth.
- Always burp your baby after every feed.
- Always keep the baby's head well supported; and never shake the baby.
- Do not apply cosmetics, or any powders and creams without your paediatrician's approval.

Before concluding I would like to tell all the mother's about one of my experiences which I had at around the same time as when I was writing this book. A mother brought her 3 weeks old baby to me saying that baby is passing blood in stools. In spite of my persistent questioning she insisted that baby is receiving only breast feeds; and nothing else. I advised her to avoid cow's milk/ buffalo's milk in her diet ; telling her that the bleeding might be due to the cow's milk protein secreted in her breast milk. Investigations were done to rule out any infection, bleeding or gut related problems.

She came to me 16 days later to tell that the bleeding has stopped. She very hesitantly informed me that she had actually started giving cow's milk to the baby from 2 weeks of age ; and that she didn't inform me about it earlier because she had done it in spite of me telling her time and again not to give cow's milk to the baby. The bleeding has stopped a few days after she stopped giving cow's milk to her baby. This experience of mine should be able to convince all the mothers to follow our advice not to introduce allergens like cow's or buffalo's milk in the baby's diet till I year of age. Not all babies develop the same problem; but let not the one baby who develops the problem be yours.

❑❑❑

Section II

Six Months to Six Years

22

Food, Water, Digestion and Excretion

Some facts about various foods that will help the mother to understand 'food and nutrition' better are:

Calories are provided by Carbohydrates (in cereals like rice, wheat etc); proteins (in pulses like red gram, Bengal gram etc, meat, fish, nuts, milk products and eggs); and fats (oils, ghee etc).

Carbohydrates form the immediate source of energy. Proteins and fat come into play when carbohydrates are used up.

Proteins are important for bone growth and muscle growth.

Fats in appropriate amounts are important for normal functioning of the body and brain.

Excessive amount of calories can lead to the problem of obesity.

Vitamins and Minerals are important for normal functioning of the body, protection from infections, good functioning of various sensory organs like eyes, good bone growth and good mental development.

Vitamin A present in carrots, papaya etc is essential for good eye sight and good skin. Deficiency of vitamin A can lead to night blindness, dryness of eyes and total loss of vision.

Vitamin B complex present in various vegetables, greens and unpolished cereals are essential for keeping the skin, lining of the gut and mouth intact, for proper functioning of various body processes, for healthy blood and healthy nerve cells.

Vitamin C present in various citrus fruits and mangoes is essential for immunity, good skin, strong gums, bones and blood vessels.

Vitamin D predominantly synthesised in the body by adequate sun exposure is very essential for strong bones.

Vitamin E in nuts is essential for good skin and proper functioning of the body.

Vitamin K is essential for good clotting of the blood and is synthesised by the bacteria residing in human gut.

Calcium in milk and egg is essential for bone growth.

Iron in greens, beans, pomegranate, jaggery, dates, honey and meat is very important for blood production. Deficiency of iron causes anaemia.

Iodine in iodinated salt is important for proper functioning of the thyroid gland and thus proper functioning of the brain. That is why it is better to use iodised salt for cooking.

Fibre in the diet is essential for good and smooth passage of stools. Fruits and vegetables are rich in fibre.

A balanced diet consisting of all these nutrients needs to be given to the child for good growth and development.

Food and Nutrition:

Diet of her child is an issue which worries every mother. Most mothers are always worried that their children do not eat well. Some mothers worry too much about their children eating too much and becoming obese. Very few mothers seem to be contended with the type and quantity of food their children eat. The most basic rule that every mother should follow is that she should periodically add newer varieties to her child's diet, and allow her child to determine what and how much he/she wants to eat. Expose the child to varieties of cereals, pulses, meats, fruits, vegetables, greens, nuts from the beginning (avoid introducing peanuts, tree nuts, egg white, sea food, cow's milk, soya, and wheat till the age of one because there is a chance that they can cause allergic conditions in the child). The child should be encouraged and allowed to feed soft finger foods from his/her plate from around 9 to 10 months of age even if he/she is going to make a big mess all around. Similarly, children should also be allowed to hold a cup and drink from it from around 9 to 10 months of age.

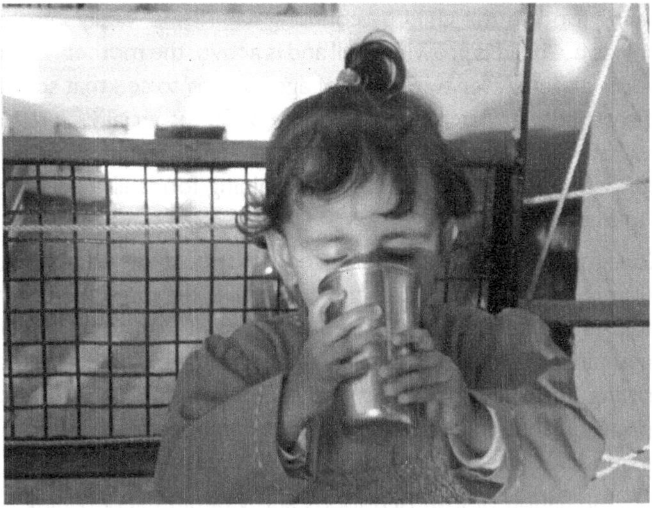

Fig: 29 Toddler drinking milk from the tumbler

Follow these tips to help your child develop healthy food habits

- From around 15 months of age let the child sit with his/her parents at the dining table and self-feed with the mothers help. Sometimes children will show an initial disliking to some foods, but will start enjoying them when you reintroduce the same after a few days; and so mothers should periodically expose them to those foods.
- Children should be allowed to have high calorie foods like chips and high sugar foods like ice creams and cakes once in a while; and too much restriction need not be placed as long as they develop good eating habits otherwise. Fat intake should not be restricted till the age of two; after which some amount of restriction is needed.
- Children should never be over stuffed and forced to finish whatever is kept in their plate; otherwise they are likely to develop an aversion to some foods and thus become anorexic. Overstuffing can also lead to the problem of obesity. Elders in the house should set an example to the child by eating healthy food themselves.
- Encourage children to play outdoors rather than spend more time in front of the television and computer. Children should be discouraged from eating snacks while watching television. This will go a long way in preventing the child from becoming obese.

- Giving food to the child by counting calories is totally impractical. As long as the child is growing well and is active, the mother has nothing to worry about. After two years of age she has to see that some amount of restriction is placed on the intake of fat; especially on the intake of saturated fats like ghee, cheese, butter, dalda etc. Some restriction on excessive intake of cholesterol containing foods like egg, meat etc is also needed.
- Consumption of milk and milk products should be restricted to around 700ml a day in young children ; otherwise the absorption of iron from their gut is likely to be impaired(especially if iron containing foods are taken at the same time as calcium containing foods like milk) and their craving for iron rich foods is likely to decrease. At the same time it is important that children take adequate amounts of milk/milk products (around 500ml a day) for the growing bones.
- A combination of iron rich foods and vitamin C containing foods will be good for better absorption of iron. Vitamin C improves the child's immunity and prevents frequent episodes of cold. Adequate exposure to sun (10 minutes of exposure for the fore arms and face between 9.00am and 3.00pm every day) is important for vitamin D synthesis by the body and thus for having strong teeth and bones. Vitamin B 12 supplementation is a must for children who are given a vegetarian diet that excludes even milk from it. A combination of milk products and iron rich foods will impair iron absorption; and so should be avoided.
- Intake of fruit juices should be restricted to about 250 ml per day in young children so as to avoid the problems of diarrhoea and bloating. Instead children should be encouraged to eat the fruits. The fibre in the fruits and vegetables is good for digestion and smooth passage of stools.
- Young children, especially toddlers do not realise that they are thirsty. It is important that mothers offer them water to drink in between meals, and during meals. Too much water should not be offered during meals; otherwise the child may feel full and will not complete his meal.
- By giving the child a variety of foods and a balanced diet, the mother will be able to give her child all the necessary nutrients, including vitamins and minerals in adequate amounts; and so will not have to give any extra tonics. Unnecessary administration of vitamin supplements esp. vitamins A, D and E can cause serious problems to the child; and so vitamin tonics should be given to the child only according to the paediatrician's prescription.

- Overcooking, deep frying and soaking for too long can lead to loss of certain vitamins from the food; and so should be avoided. Exclusively breast fed babies will need iron tonic after 4 months of age because the iron in breast milk will not be sufficient for the baby after 4 months of age. Iron supplementation can be discontinued once you start giving iron rich foods regularly. It is better to discuss this with a paediatrician. Never start iron supplementation on your own. For that matter do not give any tonics on your own without consulting a paediatrician. Toxic amounts of some vitamins and minerals can cause serious complications.
- Sprouting enhances the nutritional value of various food items. Fermentation improves the nutritional value; especially the vitamin C content. Overcooking, oversoaking and excessive polishing decreases the nutritional value, and many vitamins and minerals are lost. Parboiling of rice preserves the vitamins, especially vitamin B present in its outer coat. Unwashed and undercooked food carries the risk of infection. Keep all this in mind while preparing food.
- Avoid giving foods containing monosodium glutamate (ajinomoto or Chinese salt); especially in the first year of life. Foods like grapes, peanuts etc can be given to the child only in the presence of the parent till 4 years of age till which period the chance of choking on them is very high. It is better to give foods like pea nuts in some other more easily chewable form.

Your ?s My Answers:

My daughter is 9 months of age. She doesn't show any interest in the food I give. She seems to want to drink only milk all the time. How can I improve her appetite?

Ideally you should have started cow's milk only after she completed I year of age. Now that you have started it, continue the same. Restrict the amount of milk you give to your daughter to around 600ml to 700ml a day; otherwise too much milk will suppress her appetite for other foods, especially those rich in iron. Many babies develop anaemia (thinning of blood) due to lack of iron (iron deficiency anaemia) around this age. This can be the cause for poor appetite. Kindly talk to your paediatrician. Offer your baby a variety of foods rather than restricting her to tinned foods and milk. Your approach should be such that by the time of her first birthday she should be eating all soft foods that the family eats except for the spicy and fatty stuff. Give her things she can pick up and eat; for example, idly pieces and bread crumbs etc. Allow her to handle the spoon. Allow her to drink from the cup. Let her enjoy her meal even if she is making a mess all around. Try to wean her away from the bottle and let her drink milk from the tumbler or cup. Warm food is good for digestion and children generally eat better when served warm food. Her appetite will gradually improve if you follow the above measures consistently.

My daughter is 10 months of age. She is constipated. Tell me some home remedy.

Firstly, be sure that she is constipated. If she is passing soft stools once in 2 to 3 days, it is normal; but if she is passing hard stools and is straining to pass them then she is constipated even if she is passing stools every day. In such a case, try to give more fluids, fruits and vegetables to her. Soak few dry grapes and dry dates in water over night and give her few spoons of that water to drink in the morning. It will help her in having softer stools. Consult a paediatrician if these tips don't help her. It is important to rule out thyroid deficiency and local problems like fissure (split in the skin and muscle) in the anal area (especially if she is crying a lot to pass stools).

My son is 3 years. He keeps retching and sometimes vomits whenever I give any food item that he doesn't like. Should I give some medicine to stop that?

No, for sometime avoid giving the foods he doesn't like. Read the section on 'Food and Nutrition' to get an idea about how to develop healthy eating habits in children. Do it gradually. Reintroduce the foods you have stopped one by one after few days and see if he is going to tolerate them.

My son is 1½ years of age. He keeps having diarrhoea almost once every month. Otherwise he is active and is growing well. What should I do?

Children between 1-3 years of age have loose stools often without any particular cause. This type of diarrhoea is not severe and doesn't cause much problem. Excess of sugar containing foods and fluids and excess of fruit juices can increase the problem of loose stools and gas. Try to restrict fruit juices to around 250ml a day. Restrict sweets. Encourage him to eat fruits rather than giving fruit juices.

How do I treat my son at home if he develops diarrhoea and vomiting?

Loose stools are a common problem; and can be managed at home if it is not severe. Mostly, it is either infective or due to overfeeding and excess sugar in the foods or fluids. You can manage your son at home if the loose stools are not too frequent, he is not having fever, and is active and playful. Buy ORS (Oral Rehydration Solution) sachets from the medical shop and follow the simple instructions given on them to prepare the solution. Before buying the sachet make sure that it is WHO (World Health Organization) recommended. This will be written on the sachet. Boil water, cool it and then prepare the solution in a clean container. Discard the solution after 24 hours. You have to keep the water boiling on the stove for around 10 minutes after the bubbles appear in order to free the water from germs. Many times the common mistake made is that the stove is turned off once the bubbles appear. Give around 50 ml of this solution after every loose stool sip by sip. Let him drink as much ORS as he wants to drink. If he asks for plain water in between, let him have it. His diet should consist of freshly cooked easily digestible foods like kanji (rice water), dal water, soup, bananas etc. Restrict oils, spices, fruit juices; glucose, plain sugar and preferably milk till loose stools subside. If he is vomiting, wait for some time and try to give ORS with spoon. Give a minute or so between each spoon of ORS. If he continues to vomit, refuses to drink anything, develops frequent loose stools, becomes dull, develops fever, or starts passing very less urine do consult a paediatrician immediately. Do not try to administer antibiotics to the child whenever he has diarrhoea or vomiting. Let the paediatrician decide about it. Unnecessary administration of antibiotics can lead to death of useful organisms which reside in the gut and thus cause more problems like diarrhoea and poor absorption of nutrients later on. Some mothers tend to starve the child thinking that his loose stools will stop with that. Do not do such things. Ensure that the child gets adequate nutrition and fluids.

When and how should I stop breast feeds for my daughter 1 year of age?

Continue breast feeds till 2 years of age. After that, stop feeds gradually so that you do not develop the problems of painful breasts and dribbling of milk. If milk secretion does not stop, consult a doctor for appropriate medicines to stop milk production.

My daughter is 2 years of age. I want to stop breast feeds. How do I do it?

Stop gradually so that you do not develop the problems of breast engorgement and the embarrassing problem of milk dribbling down from your breasts. This will also be easy on your daughter. In case you have to stop abruptly for some reason talk to your doctor who would prescribe you medicines for the same.

My daughter is 6 years of age. She is complaining of stomach pain almost every day for the past 5 days. Is she suffering from some serious ailment?

Look for worms in her stools and get her treated for the same. In case her complaints have started after a recent introduction of a new food item, stop giving that food for sometime and see if her stomach pain decreases. If so, she might be allergic to that food item. Many children do this to get the attention of their parents and some do it to skip school. Encourage her to develop regular bowel habits. Give her adequate time in the toilet to empty her bowels. Try not to give attention to her complaint if she is looking well otherwise and doesn't appear to be in severe pain. If she appears to be in severe pain, do take her to a paediatrician.

My son is 4 years of age. He is very fat. How do I get him to decrease his weight?

Obesity can lead to more problems like diabetes (high blood sugar) and high blood pressure in the future. You need to ensure that he decreases his weight to an optimum level gradually, not abruptly. Start by gradually changing his dietary pattern to a healthy and balanced one. You set an example by following a good pattern yourself. Restrict foods like chips, sweets, and ice creams to once or twice a week. Also restrict aerated drinks and prepacked fruit juices. Encourage him to have vegetable salads as snacks. Try to make the salads look appetising so that he shows more interest in having them. Encourage him to eat fruits rather than drink fruit juices. Do not add extra ghee, butter and cream in his food. Meet a dietician to know about the number of calories your child would require every day. Try to keep his caloric intake to that level every day. Encourage him to play more rather than sitting in front of the TV or computer. Discourage him from snacking while watching TV. Be kind and gently explain to him the need to decrease his weight. Do not be harsh with him and never ridicule him. Make the changes in his diet gradually, and not abruptly. Encourage him by giving small gifts and tight hugs when he cooperates with you.

My son is 2 years of age. He eats mud, paper, chalks etc. What can I do to make him stop eating those things?

Eating non-nutritive substances like mud is called 'pica'. It is very commonly associated with iron deficiency anaemia (anaemia due to lack of iron). It is also commonly associated with worm infestation (worms in stools), and lead poisoning (occurs by eating wall paints, pencils etc). Your child needs to be investigated for anaemia, worms in stools, and lead poisoning and treated appropriately.

My daughter is 3 years of age. She is not growing well. She passes foul smelling bulky stools. What can I do about it?

Meet a paediatrician. She may be having deficiency of certain enzymes required for digestion and absorption of food. Her stools need to be examined. The paediatrician will advise you regarding the further course.

My son is 4 years of age. He always wants to pass stools just after meals. What can I do about it?

This reflex of passing stools is a very common thing even with adults. I don't think you should give undue importance to it. He will outgrow it with time.

My son is 2 years of age. He passed whitish stools yesterday. Is he having jaundice?

Many children pass pale stools sometimes due to indigestion. That does not imply that they are having jaundice. Consult a doctor if he is having yellowness of eyes and urine.

My 5-year-old son takes hours to finish his food. What do I do?

This problem could have been prevented from occurring in the first place. Generally young children spend more time at their plate. Parents hurry them to finish their meal because they will want to attend to other daily chores. The child finds it more and more amusing to irritate the impatient parent, and enjoys the attention he/she is getting during meal time. This habit of eating slow persists. The same must have happened with your son too. Stop telling him to finish his food fast. Do not talk about it to others in his presence. Ignore the habit completely for some time. He is likely to outgrow the habit once you start ignoring it, and he sees that the rest of the family finishes its meal and gets up from the table without bothering about his slowness.

There are white dots on my son's nails. Are they due to calcium deficiency?

White dots on some nails are common among young children. They do not really indicate anything.

My mother says that I should not give oranges and bananas to the child in winters, lest he should catch cold. Is it true?

No. Oranges are rich in vitamin C. Bananas are rich in many vitamins and minerals. Vitamin C in fact is said to improve the child's ability to fight infections.

What are antioxidants?

These are substances which prevent damage to the skin, blood vessels and various other organs of the body by oxygen free radicals. Vitamin E, Vitamin A, Vitamin C and omega 3 fatty acids etc have such properties. Adequate intake of foods containing these will help in keeping the child healthier.

My child is 4 years of age. He was born preterm. He eats vegetables only when given in a mashed form. What can I do to change his habit?

Your child preferring to eat vegetables in a mashed form has got nothing to do with his being born preterm. Encouraging children to start eating a variety of foods should start from as early as one year of age. Anyway, it is never too late! Try to keep a different vegetable in his plate every day. Be consistent about it. Do not force him to finish the helping. Just tell him to taste the vegetable and allow him to leave it if he doesn't like it. Some day, may be in a month or two, he will finish his helping all by himself. Reward him for that with a tight hug. He will gradually develop a taste for some vegetables at least! Meanwhile try to take care of his nutrition (vitamins and minerals) by giving him fruits. If he doesn't show interest in them also, you will have to give him some syrup containing vitamins and minerals till his dietary pattern improves.

Growth and Development

Growth and development of a child are those aspects about which every mother should have a basic idea. Paediatricians plot the growth of the child periodically on the growth chart. If your baby is growing appropriately it will be clearly depicted on the growth chart. Please do not go by the various numbers written in books about the weight and height of the child. Those numbers are just an average to serve as a guide to the paediatricians. Your child may be growing more than what those numbers say, or less than what those numbers say. These numbers should not bother you as long as the growth chart says that the child is growing appropriately. Do not keep comparing your child with other children. I have tried to explain about growth curves here by giving the growth curves of two boys of the same height growing appropriately, but still differing considerably in their weight. In the first growth chart, the child is following 50th percentile for his weight. In the second chart, the child is following 25th percentile for weight. Both children are following the same 50th percentile for their respective heights.

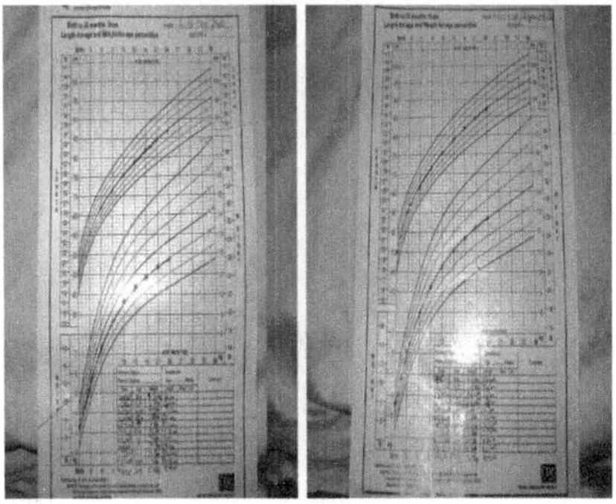

Fig: 30 Growth charts of two boys

Development occurs in the same sequence for every child, although the time at which certain milestones are attained will differ for each child. For example, all babies will have to first learn to sit before learning to stand irrespective of the age at which they attain these milestones. Mothers should be aware of this fact that some babies learn to do certain things earlier than others and some later than others. They should stop comparing their babies with other babies for each and every milestone. In the following pages I have given only a brief overview of the child's development rather than giving elaborate details about the time of attainment of various milestones because I believe that mothers should enjoy their child's development rather than checking from the book every time to see if their child is attaining all the milestones at the right time. At the end of this chapter , I have given a brief idea about the upper limits for the attainment of certain important milestones. If the child doesn't attain them even after the upper limit is crossed, a paediatrician needs to have a look at the child.

Babies start doing so many things **between 6 to 12 months of age**. They will start sitting unsupported, crawling, pulling themselves up to stand, cruising along the furniture, and some will even walk independently before their first birthday.

Most babies sit without supporting themselves on their hands by around 8 months of age.

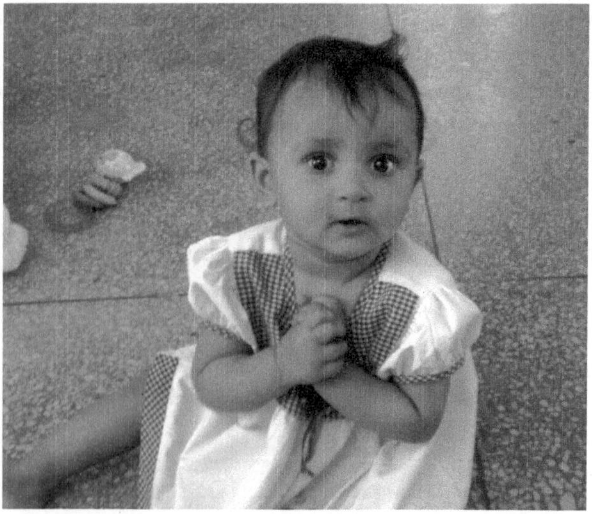

Fig: 31 Sitting unsupported

Most babies start crawling comfortably (i.e move about on their tummies) by around 8 months of age. Most babies start creeping (i.e move about supporting themselves on their hands and knees) by around 10 months of age.

Fig: 32 Creeping

Babies start pulling themselves up to stand by around 8 to 9 months of age; and in a month, or so they would start cruising along the furniture.

Fig: 33 Pulling herself up to stand

Fig:34 Cruising along the furniture

Most babies walk independently by 13 months of age.

Fig: 35 Walking independently on the first birthday

They will start saying dada, mama etc. by around 8 to 9 months of age. By 1 year of age most of them will be able to say at least 2 meaningful words; for e.g. addressing mother as 'amma' etc. They will be using their thumb and index finger to pick up objects. This is known as 'pincer grasp'. Mothers have to keep away small beads, pea nuts etc out of reach so as to prevent the child from choking on such objects and foods.

Fig: 36 2 year old child using pincer grasp to hold the crayon

They will start understanding more and more of what the parents say to them. They will start searching here and there for their toys. Mothers have to be on the look out always; otherwise there is a high chance of accidental injuries.

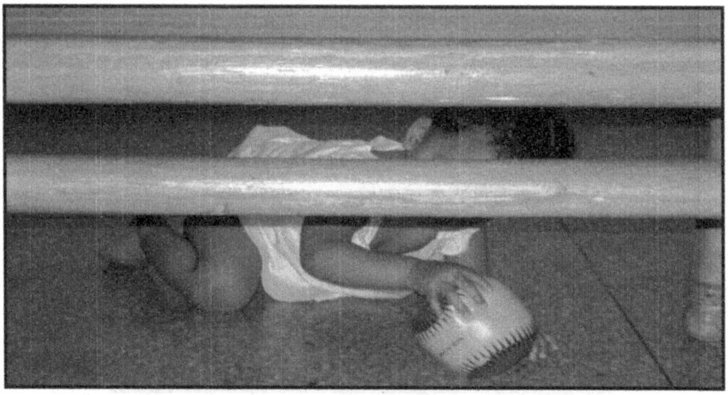

Fig:37 A toddler searching for the ball under the table
(chance of accidental injury to the head)

Keep your cameras ready to record their milestones and antics. It is going to be fun and hectic at the same time. This is the age at which babies stop going to strangers. This is also the age at which tantrums make their first appearance. So firmness in dealing with a child throwing a tantrum will have to start from the beginning itself. Mothers should encourage babies to look at the picture books more often, especially from 9 months of age. This is one of the best ways to make the baby pick up language.

Between 1 and 2 years of age; children will learn walking, running, climbing stairs, pulling toys and jumping to some extent. They will start learning more and more words so much that by their second birthday they will be making short sentences consisting of 2 words. They will enjoy scribbling and feeding themselves.

Fig:38 Enjoying feeding herself

They will enjoy playing with blocks and form boards.

Fig: 39 Enjoying putting the blocks one on top of another

Fig: 40 Manipulating the square into its place on the form board

They will enjoy playing with toys and pulling their toys.

Fig: 41 Pulling the toy

They will enjoy learning from picture books.

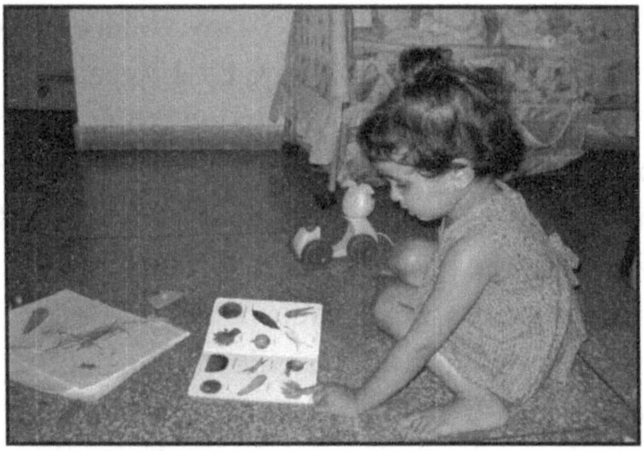

Fig: 42 Learning from picture book

They will also start informing their mother about passing urine and stools from around 15 to 18 months of age. Most importantly, they will start hugging and kissing their parents. Tantrums increase during the second part of second year. Food and sleep related problems also increase at this age. Many children keep clinging on to their parents in the second part of second year due to 'separation anxiety'; but this is a normal phenomenon and the child will outgrow it soon. This is the age at which parents can inculcate good eating habits and good sleep hygiene in their children by being consistent in what they teach to the child.

Between 2 to 5 years of age; children will improve their running, jumping and climbing skills, will start riding a tricycle, and will start hopping and then skipping as they grow up.

Fig: 43 Trying to pedal the tricycle

From around three years of age children will be able to count, tell their age and sex. Language picks up so much so that children will be speaking quite fluently by 2 ½ to 3 years of age. Many children become dry by day (i.e. do not wet their pants during the day) by 2 ½ years of age. They would have learnt to inform the parent about passing stools much before attaining day time control over urination. Parents have to be firm when the child throws a tantrum. Tantrums usually phase out by 5 years of age. Disciplining the child can start anytime between 2 to 3 years of age according to the level of understanding of the child. Picture books become very important for acquiring language. Telling them stories and encouraging them to tell stories is very important for the development of language and imagination. Problems like stuttering make their appearance during this period and should be ignored unless they persist for more than 6 months.

I will now mention about the upper limits for the attainment of certain milestones. If the child doesn't attain them even after the upper limit is crossed, a paediatrician needs to have a look at the child.

- Smiling on social contact, opening hands spontaneously, supporting himself on his forearms, cooing and laughing by 3 months of age
- Sitting momentarily, transferring objects from one hand to the other and to the mouth, babbling (ma, ba etc) by 6 months of age
- Pulling oneself up to stand, ability to hold objects using thumb and index finger by 9 months of age
- Walking with one hand held, saying at least two meaningful words by 1 year of age
- Saying at least 6 meaningful words by 1 ½ years of age
- Running, saying few two word sentences by 2 years of age

Your ?s My Answers:

My daughter is 13 months of age. She started walking on her own few days back. Her legs appear bent. Is she going to have bow legs?

Most, rather almost all babies will have some amount of bending at the legs when they start learning to walk. This will get corrected gradually; and the legs will become straighter by around two years of age. Deficiency of vitamin D and certain other diseases can cause inappropriate bowing of legs. Bow legs are also more common in certain families. It is always better to get a pediatrician's opinion.

Fig: 44 Slight bending of the legs of a toddler

My son is 11 months of age. He hasn't yet started walking by himself whereas my neighbour's daughter of the same age has already started walking all by herself. Why is it so? Is something wrong with him?

No. On an average, kids start walking all by themselves at around 13 months of age. Some may do it earlier like your neighbour's daughter; and some may even do it as late as 15 month of age. You do not have anything to worry about as long as your son's development is appropriate for his age otherwise. Get a paediatrician to assess your son's development if you are very worried.

My daughter is 2 years of age. Neighbours keep saying that she looks too thin. She is otherwise active and eats well. How do I make her chubby?

Each child has a different constitution. Do away with the notion that chubby children are healthy. Check out with your paediatrician. You don't have to worry if he/she feels that your daughter is growing well (after plotting her growth on the growth chart); especially since she is active and eating well. If she is not growing well according to the paediatrician, then you have to see where the problem lies and tackle it as per the paediatrician's advice. Most probably you have to just improve her diet. Have a look at the 'Food and Nutrition' section.

My son is 2 years of age. He says only a few words and one or two short sentences whereas my neighbour's daughter of the same age has already started talking a lot. What is the problem with him?

Some children talk earlier, and some later. I feel your son is perfectly normal. Do not worry and compare him too much with other kids. He too is going to talk a lot in few months. Get his developmental assessment done by a paediatrician if you are worried.

My daughter is 2 years of age. She keeps using 'la' for 'ra'. What should I do?

Lisping is a common thing at this age. It will get corrected as she grows up.

My 4 year old son keeps writing only the mirror images of the letters 'B' and 'C'. How do I correct him?

Be patient. It is a common problem with many kids at this age. He will learn very soon to write the alphabets the right way.

My child is 3 years of age. He stammers. How do I make him stop that?

Many children stammer at this age. Most of them outgrow it in 6 months or so. In case his stammering persists for a longer time, especially till after 5 years of age; he will require speech therapy. Till then, try to ignore it. Do not make your child more anxious by scolding him, correcting him, or ridiculing him. He is likely to outgrow it earlier if you give no attention to it.

My daughter is 1 year of age. She was born in her 8th month. She looks tiny compared to other kids of her age. Is she ever going to grow up to look like them?

Yes. Give her some more time to catch up. Most preterm babies catch up with their peers by 2 to 4 years.

My son is 4 years of age. He looks quite short compared to his friends. Both I and my husband are also short. Can I increase his height in some way?

The final height of the child depends on many factors. One important factor is the height of the parents. Talk to a paediatrician and make sure that there are no problems with his nutrition and his hormones. There is nothing much you can do to increase his height once such problems are ruled out.

Can you tell me something about children with spasticity?

These children with spasticity tend to have tightness of the muscles of the body and weakness of the muscles of the body. Some children may have only spasticity of legs and may have no other associated problem. Early detection and intervention in the form of physiotherapy and occupational therapy will help these children in overcoming their handicap to a major extent. Some children may have severe spasticity, small head, very poor IQ, developmental delay in all spheres of development, fits, difficulty in swallowing, constipation, poor growth, frequent infections, problems with passing urine, joint problems and may be mentally challenged. These children need to be managed by a special team consisting of doctors, physiotherapist, occupational therapist, psychologist and social worker to give them the best quality of life possible. Parents need to be counselled about the fact that these children cannot become like normal children and that the best possible care needs to be given to improve their quality of life. Parents also need to talk to the paediatrician about the chance of them having a second such child.

❑❑❑

24

Sleep

Developing good sleep hygiene is one of the most important aspects of child care. Certain aspects have already been discussed in the section on sleep for babies 0 to 6 months of age. In India most parents put their babies to sleep in the same bed as themselves. In such a case every precaution has to be taken by them to ensure that the baby is not harmed when they roll over or move in the bed. If one cannot be sure about it, then it is better to put the baby to sleep in a crib to start with. Generally newborns sleep up to 16 to 18 hours in a day; sleeping most of the time and waking up for brief periods in between. Gradually the duration of sleep comes down to 14 to 15 hours a day by 3 months of age; with the day time sleep coming down to 4 to 5 hours split into 3 naps. By 1 year of age total sleep comes down to 12 to 14 hours and the day time sleep comes down to 2 to 4 hours taken as 2 naps. By 1 ½ years most children take only a single nap during the day time. By 3 to 4 years most children sleep for 11 to 12 hours at night and stop taking the afternoon nap. Active and more intelligent children generally tend to sleep less.

Follow the given tips to develop good sleeping habits in your child:

- First and foremost step in developing good sleep hygiene is to put the babies in bed when they are drowsy and allow them to fall asleep all by themselves rather than putting them in the bed after they sleep off. You can rock them or sing to them till they feel drowsy. If you rock them, sing to them, or feed them till they go into deep sleep; they will expect you to do the same to put them back to sleep when they wake up at night. From the very beginning ensure that babies do not develop any such sleep associations. Allowing baby to form such associations will create sleep problems for the baby and the mother. Whenever the baby wakes up at night he/she will expect the same rocking, feeding, or singing to go back to sleep and in that process mother's sleep will also be disturbed. Almost all babies wake up at night a few times. Those babies who have learnt to fall asleep by themselves and have not developed any sleep associations will comfort themselves to go back to sleep when they wake up at night and thus the mother's sleep is not disturbed. So the parents will be fresh and ready to take good care of the baby during the day time.

- Babies should not get used to only the mother putting them to sleep. Fathers also should take an active interest in putting their babies to sleep
- Create a good atmosphere for sleeping by switching off the lights (expect the bed light), showing picture books, keeping the baby's favourite safe toy in the bed etc before putting the baby to sleep.
- You can also give the baby a nice bath with warm water before bed time. An infant (0 to 12 months) has to be put to sleep on his/her back, and never on the tummy. This is to avoid accidental suffocation and death.
- If you want the child to sleep in a separate room, ensure that the child's room and bed are safe and the child doesn't fall from the bed during sleep, or get injured due to something sharp, or doesn't get suffocated due to excessively soft bedding or ropes etc.
- Give dinner at least 1 or 2 hours before bed time. A cup of milk just before bed time is okay.
- Let the children play for some time after dinner; but let them not be too tired before going to bed. Let the house not be too noisy; but at the same time let the children get used to the household noises at least. Otherwise, they will start waking up for every small noise.
- Establish a good bed time routine. Be consistent and firm about it. Never try to force the children to sleep when they are not sleepy at all. That will only make the child resist you more, and will lead to further sleep problems. The child will feel more secure, and will give the parents less problems if he/she is happy during the day.

Your ?s My Answers:

My son is 1½ years of age. He always needs me to rock him for falling asleep. Is there any other easier way to make him fall asleep?

Whenever he wakes up in the middle of the night I have to rock him to make him go back to sleep.

You are facing this problem because you have got your son used to getting rocked for falling asleep. You have to gradually and consistently wean him of this habit. Otherwise you will have disturbed sleep, and thus feel extremely tired during the day time. Try giving him his favourite safe toy to hug every time you put him to bed. When you feel that he is sleepy, put him in bed, show him some picture books and give him his toy to hug, and then switch off the lights. Be with him till he falls asleep. Do not panic if he cries and asks you to rock him. Be firm; but of course do not let him cry for long. After 3-4 days, he will understand that you are not going to rock him to put him to sleep. He won't expect you to rock him when he wakes up in the middle of the night because he has learnt to fall asleep by himself.

My son is 1 ½ years of age. He wakes up at night at least twice to drink milk. Is it okay?

Most probably you give him milk every night just before he sleeps. In that case, he would have started associating his sleep with drinking milk. That is why he wants to drink milk to go back to sleep whenever he wakes up at night. Try to wean him off this habit by following steps similar to what I have written in the previous answer. Some kids get used to drinking milk at night even though they are not hungry because parents get them used to that habit by giving milk every time they wake up at night thinking that they are hungry. Generally kids don't feel hungry at night after the age of 3 to 6 months if they are fed adequately during their dinner.

My daughter 4 years of age goes to bed only at 12.00 am. She resists if I try to put her to bed early. What should I do?

It is not too late to regularise her sleep. Enforce strict bed time routine.

Let the atmosphere at home be quiet and relaxing before bed time. Discourage her from watching TV and playing active sports just before bed time. Encourage her by giving small gifts whenever she goes to bed on time. You will be able to make her establish a good sleep routine.

My daughter is 3 years of age. She goes to sleep at around 9 pm every night. Many times she wakes up between 10 pm and 11pm screaming and crying. She becomes more agitated if we try to console her. She goes back to sleep by herself within a few minutes. What can be the problem with her?

Your daughter is waking up because of what we term as 'night terrors'. Do not try to wake her up during that time. This problem is seen with quite a few young children. They generally outgrow this problem as they grow older. There really is nothing much that we can do about it. Do not worry about it. Learn to cope up with the stress for some time.

My daughter is 3 years of age. She walks in her sleep. Is there something I can do to stop that?

Sleep walking is a common problem with many young children. You would have observed that she does this at about 1 or 2 hours after going to sleep. She is going to outgrow her problem as she grows older. Make the house accident proof so as to ensure that she doesn't injure herself when she walks in her sleep. She will be completely unaware that she is walking in her sleep. Do not try to wake her up. Bring her back safely to her bed and allow her to continue with her sleep.

My son is 5 years of age. He gets frequent nightmares, usually in the early morning. He wakes up crying. He goes back to sleep after a lot of cajoling. Can we do something about it?

Nightmares are a problem not just with children. Even adults have nightmares. The problem is that your son is able to recollect a part of his dream when he wakes up. That is why he goes back to sleep only after a lot of cajoling. Calm him and put him back to sleep. Make his bed time more pleasant. Talk to him about his school, his friends etc. Try to remove any stress he may be facing at home, or at school.

My daughter is 10 months of age. Sometimes she sits up in her sleep and bangs her head. Sometimes she keeps rocking her body too. What is the problem with her?

This phenomenon does occur in many normal children at this age. She will outgrow it in 1 or 2 years. Make sure that the bed is safe so that she doesn't injure herself in the process.

My daughter is 7 months of age. She keeps rolling her head on the bed. She has lost all the hair present at the back of her head. I am worried.

Head rolling does occur with many kids at this age. She is going to stop it in one or two years. The hair is going to grow back anyway.

My son is one and a half years of age. He grinds his teeth during his sleep. What is the problem with him? Will it affect his teeth in some way?

This is known as 'bruxism'. It is a relatively common problem with young children. It is said that some children relieve their daytime anxiety and stress by grinding their teeth at night. Try to relieve your son's daytime anxiety. You might be forcing him to eat what he doesn't like to, or might be forcing him to toilet train. Try to see that there is no inconsistency in the way either parent handles him from time to time. Do not force him to go to bed. Take him to bed when he feels sleepy. Tell him some story, or sing a song and make his bedtime enjoyable. Allow him to comfort himself to sleep by hugging his favourite safe toy. Some times 'bruxism' can occur without any reason. Wait for him to outgrow the habit. If it is severe, get a dentist's opinion to rule out damage to his teeth.

❑❑❑

25

Teeth

Generally first milk tooth erupts at around 6 months of age. It may be delayed even up to 13 months of age in some babies and in some families without any apparent reason. All the 20 milk teeth erupt by 20 to 30 months of age. Permanent teeth erupt from around 6 years of age. All permanent teeth will erupt by 17 to 20 years of age. In any case, if there is delay in the eruption of teeth, paediatrician's opinion is needed to rule out problems like lack of thyroid hormone and vitamin D.

Follow the given tips for taking care of the teeth of your child:

- Care of the teeth can start just before the eruption of milk teeth. After feeding the baby, gums and tongue can be wiped clean with a wet, soft and clean cotton cloth.

  One can continue doing the same once the teeth start erupting.

- Brushing of teeth can start when sufficient teeth have appeared i.e. from around 1 year of age. Tooth brushes which are appropriate for the child's age, and have soft nylon bristles can be used. Teeth need to be brushed at least twice a day; especially once before bed time. Parental supervision is a must till 4 years of age. It is easier for the parent to brush the child's teeth by standing behind the child and tilting his head slightly backwards.

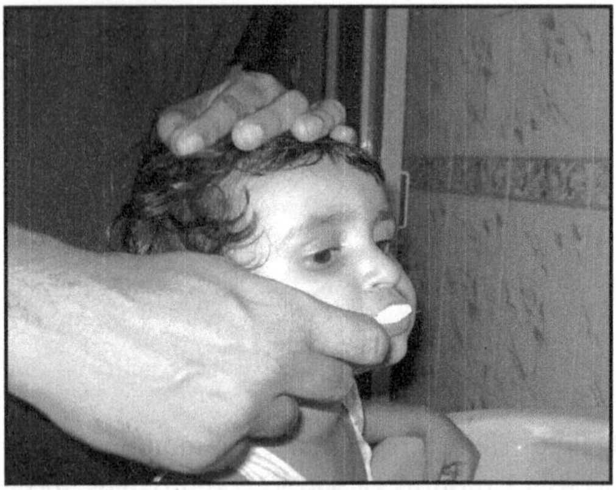

Fig: 45 Father brushing the teeth of a toddler

Parents have to help the child in brushing thoroughly till he/she is 6 to 7 years of age.

- Till 4 years of age, only a pea-sized amount of tooth paste has to be put on the tooth brush because young children have a tendency to swallow the tooth paste; and excessive fluoride (present in the tooth paste) can cause a condition called fluorosis which can adversely affect the child's teeth and bones. At the same time lack of appropriate amount of fluoride can cause tooth decay. That is the reason why almost all the tooth pastes available in the market are fluoridated. Nowadays in most places fluoride content is appropriate in the drinking water supplied by the authorities; but still parents should make an effort to find out about it so that the problems due either to excessive fluoride or to lack of fluoride are avoided. Talk to the dentist in your area. Follow the dentist's recommendations with regard to using fluoridated/non-fluoridated tooth pastes for young children who have a tendency to swallow the tooth paste.
- There is something called floss available in the medical shops. Flossing of teeth using that can be done for older kids periodically. This is very effective in cleaning those areas where tooth brushes are not able to reach.
- The child also needs to be trained to rinse the mouth every time after eating food or drinking milk, juices etc so that harmful bacteria do not grow to cause tooth decay (caries).

- Periodic dental checkups starting from I year of age are important. Using bottles and sippy cups for drinking anything other than for drinking water will increase the risk of tooth decay. So it is better to get the child used to drinking from the tumbler or cup from the beginning.

Your ?s My Answers:

My daughter is 7 months of age. She is very irritable and lot of saliva is drooling from her mouth for the past few days. What is the problem with her?

It is most likely that her teeth are going to erupt soon. What an exciting moment for the parents! It must be paining and itching for her in the mouth. Try to give her something cold to chew upon. Teethers are available in the market for the same purpose. You have to keep the teether in the fridge (not the freezer) for some time and then give it to her to chew upon.

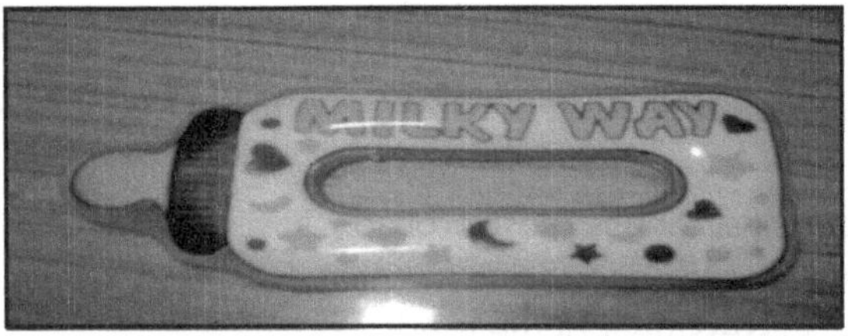

Fig: 46 Teether

You can also give vegetables like carrot etc to chew upon. These measures will help in decreasing her discomfort and irritability.

Does teething cause diarrhoea?

People have a tendency to attribute fever, diarrhoea etc to teething. Do not go with the notion that teething is responsible for these illnesses. Most of the times, it is just a coincidence.

My son is 9 months of age. He still hasn't got his first tooth. Why?

Many babies get their first tooth at around 6-7 months. Some babies may have delayed eruption of teeth due to various factors like deficiency of vitamin D, decreased thyroid hormone in the body etc. Sometimes delayed eruption of teeth may just be a feature common to one's family. Meet a paediatrician and get treatable conditions ruled out. If your baby is not having any problems with her vitamin and hormonal status, you need not be surprised even if it takes up to 13 months for his first tooth to erupt.

My son is 3 years of age. All his central upper teeth have turned black. What should I do?

Your son has developed something called 'baby bottle tooth decay' which occurs more commonly in children who continue to drink milk from bottle even after one year of age, in those who use sippy cup for drinking milk, fruit juice etc, and in those who snack frequently. Show him to a dentist. Follow the dentist's advice, encourage him to drink milk, fruit juice etc from a tumbler, practice good dental hygiene as I have mentioned in the section on dental care, and discourage frequent snacking to prevent further damage to the teeth.

My daughter is 7 years of age. She has buck teeth. All the teeth appear crowded. What should I do?

Consult a dentist. He/she would advise you appropriately. Do not ignore the problem.

My daughter is complaining of tooth ache for the past few days. What do I do?

Consult a dentist. She is most probably having caries of that tooth. She will need medicines for decreasing the pain. Further treatment will depend on the dentist's assessment of the tooth.

❑❑❑

Mouth

Queries regarding the teeth have been addressed to in the previous chapter. Certain other queries regarding 'mouth' will be addressed to in the following pages.

Your ?s My Answers:

My son is 3 years of age. He has tongue tie. When do I get him operated?

Tongue tie is not much of a problem if it is not severe. It may be responsible for some indistinctness of speech only if it is very severe. It can be operated once the child is 2 to 3 years of age. Meet a paediatric surgeon and he would operate if the tongue tie is severe.

My daughter is 9 months of age. She keeps drooling saliva. Is it normal?

Usually drooling of saliva stops by 5 to 6 months. Some babies continue to drool saliva even till 13 to 15 months of age for no apparent reasons. One of the common causes for drooling is irritation of gums caused by erupting teeth. Making her chew on a teether will help in such a case. Clean the saliva from around the mouth with a soft cotton cloth; and apply Coconut Oil or Vaseline so as prevent her from developing a skin rash or skin infection around the mouth.

My daughter has black spots on her tongue. Is it normal?

Yes. Nothing to worry about. They are nothing but enlarged taste buds.

My son has grayish patches on the tongue. Is it normal?

Yes. It is called geographic tongue. These patches meet up with each other and the entire big patch looks like a map. That is why it is called 'geographic tongue'. Consult a paediatrician once to get a better idea about it.

There is foul smell emanating from my son's mouth. What do I do about it?

Foul smell can be due to poor oral hygiene or due to foods like onions, eggs etc. Secretions from the nose can drip down the throat and cause foul smell. Let a paediatrician have a look to find the cause. He can be treated accordingly.

❑❑❑

Eyes, Nose and Ears

There are many common problems associated with these sensory organs. In the following pages, I tried to answer most of the common problems associated with these important organs of the human body.

Your ?s My Answers:

My son is 5 years of age. I have short sight. Is my son also going to have short sight? I give him plenty of carrots to eat.

Your son too has a chance of developing short sight. Is he complaining of head ache while looking at the black board? Anyway it is better to get him examined by an eye doctor (ophthalmologist) periodically; may be every 6 months to 1 year or so. Short sight is due to excessive convexity of the eye ball. Vitamin A doesn't help in reducing the convexity. Therefore do not think that by giving plenty of carrots to eat you are going to prevent him from developing short sight. Nevertheless you should continue giving him good amounts of vitamin A containing vegetables and fruits because vitamin A is essential for sharper vision and good night vision.

My son has squint. What should I do?

Some types of squint do not cause any problem with vision; whereas some cause problems with vision. Some types can result in gradual loss of vision from one eye. Some types of squint may be associated with other problems of the eye, nerves, brain etc. It is imperative that you meet an eye specialist and get your son thoroughly examined.

My daughter bleeds from the nose frequently. What should I do?

Look at the 'First Aid' section to know what to do when she bleeds from the nose. Meet the paediatrician and the ENT doctor to rule out conditions like high blood pressure and foreign body in the nose etc. Discourage your child from nose picking.

My son is 2 years of age. He keeps getting cold frequently. How do I treat him at home?

Is he sneezing frequently? If so his cold is due to allergy to dust, pollen etc. Meet a paediatrician to get appropriate medicine. Keep the house dust free and avoid exposure to pollen if the problem is severe. Instill Normal Saline nasal drops (2 drops in each nostril) at least 4 times a day to relieve his nose block. Keep him in your lap on his back and hold his head slightly lower than the rest of the body for instilling the drops. Hold him like that for a few seconds after instilling the drops.

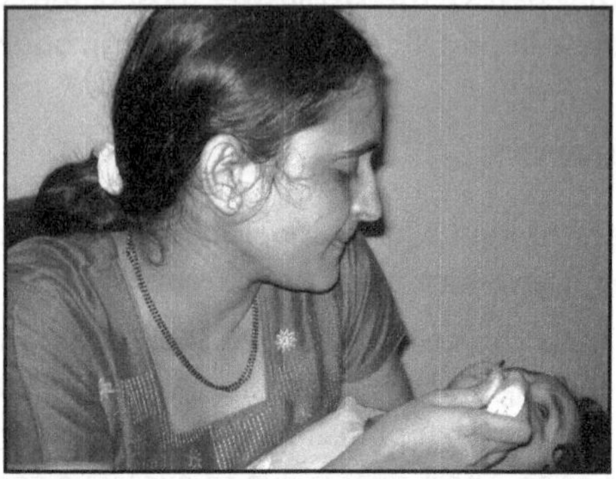

Fig: 47 Instilling nasal drops

Observe if he is breathing with his mouth when he is free of cold also. If so he might be having adenoids i.e. enlarged tonsils behind the nose. Meet an ENT doctor in such a case.

Do not keep giving antibiotics by yourself unnecessarily without a paediatrician's prescription for conditions like common cold.

My son sleeps with his mouth open. He even snores some times. He gets cough and cold very frequently. What do I do about it?

He is most probably having an enlargement of adenoids (tonsils behind the nose). Consult an ENT specialist and get him treated before the problem worsens.

How do I get rid of wax from my son's ears?

Wax from the ears gets expelled periodically by itself. You don't have to do anything about it unless it is very hard. In that case you can buy ear drops for dissolving the wax and instill them in both the ears. Let the child lie on the bed in such a way that the ear in which drops have to be instilled is facing upwards. Pull the child's ear lobe down and back to straighten the ear canal.

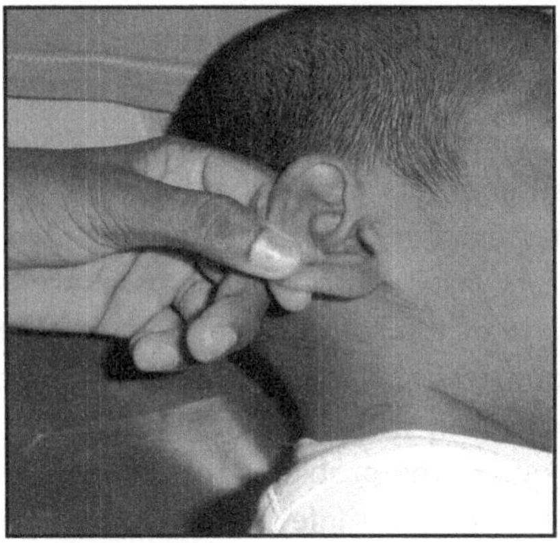

Fig: 48 Technique of straightening the ear canal by pulling the ear down, out and backwards

Instill 2 or 3 drops, close the ear flap and let the child remain in that position for a minute or two till the drops get absorbed.

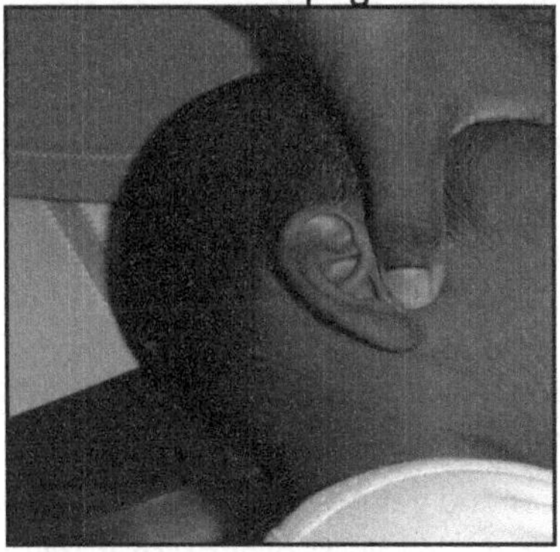

Fig: 49 Technique of closing the ear flap after instilling the ear drops

The wax will automatically be expelled out once it becomes soft. You should wash your hands with soap and water and dry them before instilling the drops. Do not touch the tip of the dropper with your hand. Do not try to remove the wax using safety pins and hair pins; otherwise you may puncture the ear drum.

How should I remove an insect that gets into my son's ear?

Do not try to remove any foreign object that gets into the ear all by yourself. Let an ENT specialist do it.

Whenever my daughter develops cold she also complains of ear pain. What can be the problem?

There is a tube connecting the ear to the nose. Whenever your daughter develops cold this tube gets blocked; thus making the ear stuffy and painful. The ear may even get infected if proper care is not taken. Treat the cold appropriately. Instill Normal Saline nasal drops in the nostrils as I have explained in one of the previous answers to relieve the nose block. Subsequently the stuffiness and pain of the ear will decrease. Whenever a young child cries excessively without being able to tell you what the problem is, then ear pain is one of the problems that you should immediately think of. The child might be having ear infection; and needs immediate treatment. Ear infection should never be neglected; otherwise it may result in deafness.

There is watery discharge from my son's ear for the past 1 month. What do I do?

Meet an ENT doctor immediately. He/she will advise you appropriately. He is most probably having an ear infection and also a hole in his ear drum. Plug his ears with cotton during bath so as to avoid water from going in.

My son had ear infection last month. Doctor said there is a small hole in his ear drum. Will he become deaf?

No. Most of these small holes heal by themselves. Large holes may need further treatment.

My daughter is 9 months of age. She doesn't respond to sounds many times. What should I do?

Meet an ENT doctor and get her hearing assessed. Any treatable problem needs to be tackled at the earliest; otherwise it will be difficult for her to learn speech later on.

How do I ensure that my daughter's ears do not pain during flight journey?

Plug her ears with cotton. Make her chew upon something during take off and landing.

❑❑❑

Skin, Scalp and Hair

A child's skin is very delicate and is prone to develop many kinds of infections, boils, rashes etc. Dryness of skin is a very common problem. Lice infestation is a very common problem with children. Queries regarding some such common problems have been answered in the following chapter.

Follow these tips for taking care of your child's's skin, scalp and hair:

Applying coconut oil or olive oil and massaging the child's body and scalp one hour before bath (including head bath) everyday will keep the child's skin, scalp, and hair in good condition. Low alkaline mild soap needs to be used for bathing children. Shampoos too have to be the mild variety. Creams (non scented) can be applied to the body immediately after towelling when the skin is still moist so that the moisture is retained and the child's skin stays soft and supple. This is especially important for kids who are prone to develop problems due to dry skin. In summers powders can be applied over the neck, under the arms and such areas where friction is maximum. This is to decrease the friction, and thus the chance of discomfort and skin rash. Do not apply powders on the face or in areas of prickly heat because powders can block the sweat pores and further aggravate the problem.

Try not to use cosmetics. Always check by applying on a small area on the hand before applying any new cream or powder on the child's face because some children may have allergy to some of the products.

Good clothing is important. Comfortable and soft clothing is required. Tight clothing has to be avoided.

Combs should not be shared. Treatment for lice infestation has to be given as soon as you notice lice in your child's hair.

Always ensure that areas like arm pits, finger webs, neck, groin etc are dry so as to prevent rashes and skin infections like ring worm. Feet need good care. Creams have to be applied to the undersurface of the feet to prevent them from cracking. Lips should be kept moist by applying ghee or coconut oil etc.

Keep the genital area clean and dry.

- **Good nutrition, sleep and adequate water intake** are very important for good skin and good hair. Always choose non-perfumed skin and hair care products especially for young children. The lesser the chemicals, the better.

Your ?s My Answers:

What do I do for 'prickly heat'?

Applying soothing lotions like Calamine will help to relieve the itching associated with prickly heat. Applying powder on the face will not help in reducing the rash; but applying powder will definitely help in reducing the friction when applied under the arms, at the elbows, on the neck etc. Put loose fitting cotton wear for the child.

My son is 5 years of age. He has whitish patches on his face. What should I do?

This is a common problem with many school going kids. It is called 'pityriasis alba'. Get a paediatrician's opinion once to rule out skin infections. Dryness of skin can increase his problem. Apply some good cream to his face if he has dry skin. Encourage him to eat good amounts of fruits and vegetables.

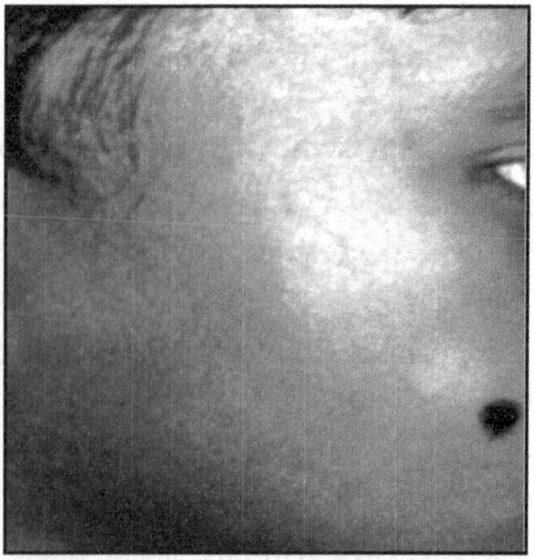

Fig: 50 Pityriasis alba

My daughter is 6 years of age. She has lots of lice in her hair. How do I get rid of them?

Please buy 1% Permethrin and apply it over her scalp taking care that nothing gets into her eyes. Shampoo it off after 1 hour. Repeat the same process after a week. Anti-lice shampoos are also available in the market. You can try using them. Ensure that the child does not accidentally drink any of these chemicals.

My son is 5 years of age. He gets boils near his nose and over his face frequently. What should I do?

This type of skin infection is a common problem in young children. Meet a paediatrician for appropriate treatment. Add dettol in a bucket of warm water and let him bathe with the same every day. Teach him not to touch his boils again and again. Try to teach him to wash his hands with soap and water whenever he touches the infected areas so as to prevent further spread of the infection.

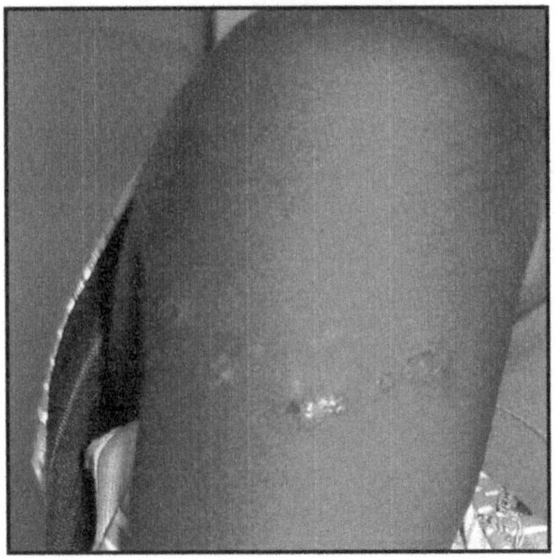

Fig: 51 Boils on the arm of a child

What is scabies?

It is an infestation of the lower layers of skin by the scabies mite. The infested child will have extreme degrees of itching and small mosquito bite like eruptions all over the body; especially on the hands and buttocks. Usually face is not involved. It is extremely infectious. It spreads by skin to skin contact and through clothes and linen. The entire family needs to be treated. Do not self-diagnose or self-treat. Always consult the doctor. If anybody in the family develops scabies, his/her clothes, linen etc should be washed thoroughly and dried in the sun. Other family members should not share the clothes and linen till treatment is complete.

What is ring worm?

It is a type of fungal skin infection which usually affects sweaty and unclean areas. The lesions look like a ring with central depression.

Many skin ointments are available in the medical shops to treat it. The tendency is to stop treatment once the lesion disappears; but ointment needs to be applied for a little longer time. Consult a dermatologist if you suspect that your child has ring worm infection.

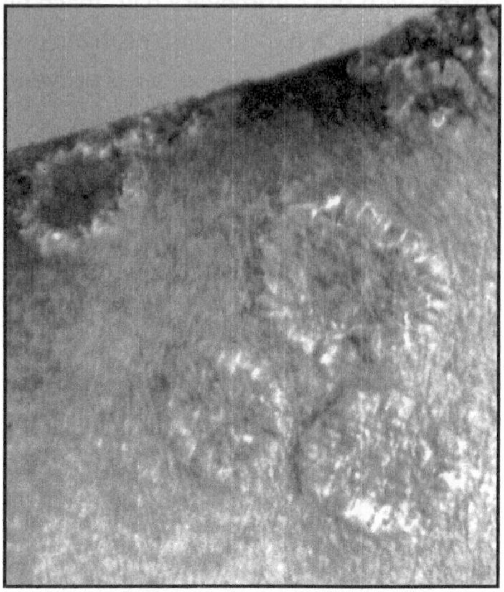

Fig: 52 Ring worm

❑❑❑

29

Genitalia

Questions about genitalia can range from queries regarding the size of the genitalia, tight foreskin, absent testis etc to problems like kids touching the genitalia often. I tried to answer few such queries here.

Your ?s My Answers:

My son is 3 years of age. He keeps touching his genitalia. I find it very embarrassing.

It is a normal phenomenon at this age. Do not panic. Do not keep scolding him for that. Instead try to divert him with something interesting like his toys, picture books etc.

My son's one testis looks larger than the other. He also has a swelling in the groin which keeps increasing in size when he cries. What should I do?

A paediatric surgeon needs to assess your son. It is likely that he is having a hernia. He may require a surgery for the same. He may also be having accumulation of fluid around his testis.

My son's testis disappears sometimes when I bathe him. Is it okay?

It is moving up due to a reflex which occurs due to stimulation of the inner aspect of the thigh. It is nothing abnormal.

I am not able to pull back my son's foreskin for the purpose of cleaning. He is 10 months of age.

Never try to forcibly pull back the foreskin. You may end up creating serious complications. Foreskin may take longer time to separate from the terminal part of the penis in many infants and toddlers.

❑❑❑

30

Bladder, Bowels and Toilet Training

Generally kids start becoming aware of passing stools and urine at an average age of 15 to 18 months. Of course, some may become aware of it earlier; and some later. They will start playing with their stools and urine. Parents can plan for toilet training after this stage in the child's development. Prior to this stage, when kids are taken to the toilet after food or after drinking water, they generally pass urine. By doing so the child gets conditioned to pass urine whenever he/she is taken to the toilet periodically; and so wet pants can be prevented to some extent. Similarly, children generally get the urge to pass stools after a meal; and so putting the child on the potty after a meal may help in decreasing the number of soiled pants. All this is not part of regular toilet training. Toilet training starts only after the child starts becoming aware of passing urine and stools.

Most kids are potty trained by around 2 years of age; and many of them as early as 18 months. They are able to inform the mother that they want to pass stools, and will be able to hold it till they reach the potty. Most of them stop wetting their pants during the day time by around 2 ½ years of age. Night time bladder control occurs only after this. Usually, most girls stop wetting their beds at night at the latest by 4 years of age and most boys by 5 years of age.

Follow the given tips to toilet train your child:

- One can start toilet training the kid by allowing him/her to watch the parents when they use the toilet. Whenever the child passes stools empty them in the potty and flush them out allowing the child to witness the whole process. The child will gradually understand that potty is the place for passing stools.
- A similar approach of squeezing the child's urine from the mopping

cloth into the potty can make the child aware of the fact that potty is the place for passing urine too. Allow the child to mop up the urine if he/she wants to.

- Special potties are available for young kids. Special potty seats which can be placed on the regular potty are also available in the market. Either of them can be purchased for the child so that the child is more comfortable while using the potty.

Fig: 53 Potty

Fig: 54 Potty seat for kids

- One can start putting the child on the potty seat whenever it looks like the child is going to pass stools as evident from his/her expressions. Do not force the child if the child offers resistance. Give a break for few days and restart the toilet training process. No child can be forcefully toilet trained. Let the potty training exercise be a pleasant one for the child. Mother can sing, talk and tell stories while the child is at the job.

Allow the child to play with the flush and other harmless bathroom fittings and become familiar with the place. Gradually the children will learn to control their urge till you put them on the potty. Initially they will want to go to the potty fast; but after some time this kind of urgency decreases. They will start giving you sufficient time for taking them to the potty.

- Encouraging the child by showing your appreciation in the form of a hug or a peck on the cheek will help a lot. Similarly, children also learn to control the urge to urinate as they grow older so much so that many of them are dry during the day by 2 ½ years of age.

Most important cause for failure to toilet train a kid in most cases is that mothers try to rush their kids into toilet training; and start becoming impatient and irritated if they don't train fast. They tend to even punish the child. If mothers learn to be more relaxed and let things take their natural course, the child will be toilet trained earlier than when mothers get too anxious to rapidly toilet train their children. Use of diapers can also delay the process because it is easier for the child to piss in the diapers rather than going to the potty to do the same.

Your ?s My Answers:

My son is 4 years of age. He wets his bed almost every night. What should I do about it?

Boys, in general, take longer to be dry at night. Some may take even up to 5 years of age. Do not worry. He is likely to stop wetting his bed on a regular basis by the age of five.

My son is 6 years of age. He continues to wet his bed at night. How do I make him stop doing that?

Your son should have attained bladder control by now. Some children take longer than the others. One positive thing is that he is not wetting his pants during the day time; and so it is unlikely that he may be having some problem with his urinary tract. He needs your help the utmost. Make bed time more enjoyable and relaxed for him. Avoid fluids 30 minutes to 1 hour before bedtime. Make him use the toilet just before going to bed. Wake him up once for urinating; around two to three hours after he goes to bed. Do not keep waking him up in the night for the same. Reward him with praise and a tight hug in the morning if he hadn't wet his bed in the night. Do not reprimand him for wetting his bed. Love and encouragement will definitely help him in overcoming this problem.

My daughter is 6 years of age. She continues to wet her bed at night. She wets her pants during the daytime too; almost once a day. What should I do? I am very worried.

Your daughter, ideally should have stopped wetting her pants by now. You should consult a paediatrician. Urine infection and abnormalities of urinary tract need to be ruled out. Constipation and worm infestation need to be ruled out. This is a very delicate issue. You have to be very careful in handling it. Do not nag her, or punish her for it. Make the atmosphere at home less stressful for her. Ensure the same at school. May be you can take her teacher into confidence. Encourage her to use the toilet more frequently during the daytime; and not wait till her bladder is full. Also encourage her to empty her bladder completely each time. I suggest that you make her use sanitary napkins during the daytime till the problem gets resolved. Thus, embarrassment in front of her peers can be avoided. Once it is established that there is no problem with her urinary tract, and there is no constipation or worm infestation; you may have to consult a child psychiatrist and take his/her advice regarding handling this problem. Follow the tips I have given in the previous answer. Let the paediatrician decide if your child needs any medication for the problem.

My daughter is 6 years of age. She had been dry at night from 3 years of age till 3 months ago. She is wetting her bed almost every night for the past 3 months. What can be the problem with her? How do I tackle it?

Your child had attained bladder control initially. She started wetting her bed again almost 2 to 3 years after attaining initial bladder control. Urine infection, constipation, and worm infestation need to be ruled out. Talk to her and try to find out if she is facing any stressful situation at school, or with peers, or at home. Help her tackle it. Allay all her fears. Make the atmosphere at home pleasant. Parents should not fight or argue in front of the child. There should not be any inconsistency in the way parents handle the child; i.e. there shouldn't be any discrepancy in the way either parent handles her. Always be consistent in what you teach her so that you do not confuse her little mind and add to the stress. I am sure your child will overcome her problem very soon with good care, encouragement, and appropriate treatment.

My son is 5 years of age. He continues to soil his pants even now. It causes him a lot of embarrassment. How do I help him?

Your son shouldn't be soiling his pants at this age. Is your child suffering from constipation? In such a case relieving him of his constipation will help him to overcome his problem. Children who are constipated tend to retain their stools till it becomes so much that the stools overflow and cause them to soil their pants. Soak some dry grapes and dry dates in water overnight. Every morning, give him some of that water to drink. This will help him in relieving his constipation, and have regular bowel movements every morning. If this doesn't help, discuss with a paediatrician for other treatable causes of this problem being faced by your son.

My son is 2 years of age. He is passing red-coloured urine for the past 2 days. What should I do about it?

Many food stuffs like beet root and some medicines can cause the urine to be coloured. Anyway it is better to get a paediatrician's opinion to ensure that there is no other problem.

My 2 year old daughter keeps getting urine infection. What should I do?

Urine infection is more common among girls because their urethra (the duct from which urine comes out) is very short and is closer to the anus than in boys. So the bacteria from the stools can reach the urethra easily and can cause infection. Always clean her genital area from front to back after she passes stools so that stool matter does not come in contact with the urethra. Use wet tissue to clean the area; or at least take care not to splash water. Meet a paediatrician if she continues to get urine infection. She may need to be investigated for problems in her urinary tract. There may be a need to keep her on daily antibiotics till she is 5 to 6 years of age. Detailed discussion about this is beyond the scope of this book.

My son is 2 years of age. He had urine infection twice this year. What should I do?

Urine infection is not common among boys. Your son needs to be investigated for problems in his urinary tract. Meet a paediatrician and discuss the problem with him/her.

❑❑❑

Fever, Infection and Infestation

Every parent should have a basic idea about prevention of infection and should be able to take the necessary measures to protect the child from various infections. Basic idea about treatment of fever at home and the problems associated with poorly controlled fever is also a must.

Follow the given tips to protect your child from infections and infestations:

- For adequate protection, drinking water should be boiled for 10 minutes after the bubbles appear. One can also use the water from water purifiers like aqua guard etc for drinking purpose.
- Food should be adequately cooked. Undercooked food can be responsible for infections and worm infestations. When preparing salads, vegetables and fruits should be washed thoroughly and peeled.
- Thorough hand washing with soap and water before eating food and after using the toilet is a must.
- Bathroom handles etc are to be periodically cleaned with disinfectant solution. Toilets have to be cleaned every day with disinfectant solutions.
- All the drains, drainage pipes and dust bins have to be cleaned with disinfectant solution every day.
- Keep the house cockroach and fly free.
- Keep the house mosquito free to protect your child from malaria, dengue, brain fever etc.
- Whenever anybody in the family has flu, cold, cough etc it is better to keep the kids at a distance. Cover with your hand if you are going to sneeze or cough. Thorough hand washing after that and after cleaning

the nose is a must. Hand kerchiefs, towels, tumblers etc need to be kept separate till the infected person becomes well.

- All children need to be vaccinated appropriately as per the advice of their paediatrician.
- Whenever the child is taken to a hospital for any purpose, ensure that disposable needles are used for injections, suturing etc. It is preferable to have one's own nebuliser set in case the child is asthmatic.
- If the mother has infections like hepatitis B and HIV, it is a must to inform the doctor so that all precautions are taken during and after the delivery to prevent the baby from acquiring it.
- If any body in the family has a skin infection, they have to be treated. Till then, kids should not be allowed to touch the infected areas or share clothes, bedding etc.
- Regular bath with soap and water , adequate towelling to prevent moistness in areas like neck and arm pits will prevent infections like ring worm.
- Regular care of the hair and keeping it lice free is very important.
- If the child is prone to develop frequent boils, putting a little bit of dettol in his bath water will help to prevent that.
- Overcrowding in the houses has to be avoided.
- Cleaning the genital area from front to back after using the toilet, especially in a girl child is very important to prevent urinary infections.
- Frequent change of diapers is important to prevent infections in the diaper area.
- Cutting nails periodically is important.
- Children should not be allowed to play with unvaccinated pets, or sick pets, or stray animals.
- Good nutrition is very important for improving the child's immunity. This will increase the child's ability to fight infection. Vitamin C is supposed to protect against frequent respiratory and urinary infections.
- Cleaning the wound thoroughly with soap and water after an injury is an important step in preventing infection.

Your ?s My Answers:

My son 3 years of age has worms in his stools. How do I treat him?

Consult a paediatrician. Give your son the medicine prescribed by him. You can deworm him every 6 months in the same way till he is able to consistently practise hand washing after using the toilet and before eating food. Some worms can make him lose small amounts of blood in stools every day. Get his blood tested for anaemia. He will need treatment with iron containing tonics in such a case.

Is it true that eating more sweets is responsible for the child developing worms in the stools and boils on the body?

Not at all! Sweets can be responsible for the decay of teeth if proper dental hygiene is not adhered to.

How do I check my daughter's temperature?

You can buy a thermometer from a nearby medical shop. It is preferable to check the temperature by keeping it in the arm pit till the child is at least 4 to 5 years of age when she is likely to understand that she is not supposed to bite the thermometer. Ensure that the tip is in contact with the skin, and not the clothing.

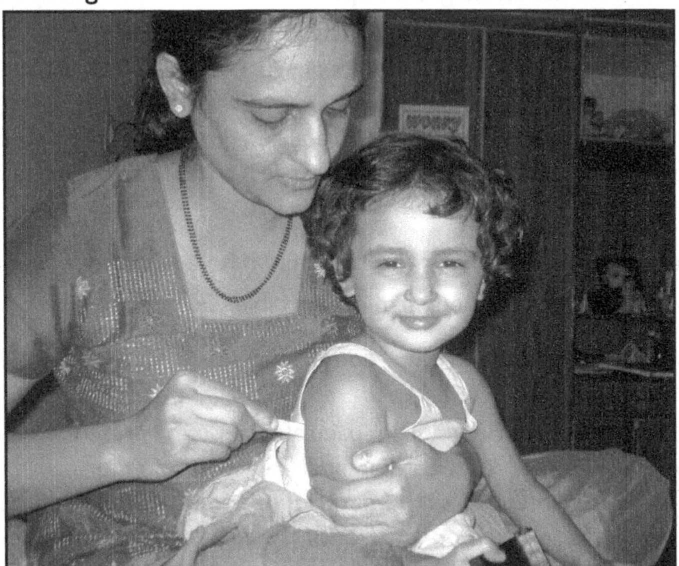

Fig: 55 Measuring temperature by keeping the thermometer tip in the arm pit

For an older child, temperature can be recorded by keeping the mercury tip of the thermometer under the tongue and asking the child to close her mouth. ***Do not leave your child alone while taking her temperature.***

Check the reading after 2 minutes. Digital thermometers which beep after the temperature is recorded are also available. If the temperature is more than 99 degrees F your child is likely to be having fever.

How do I treat fever at home?

Fever can be controlled at home by giving the child syrup paracetamol in the dose that is given on the label. High fevers can sometimes precipitate fits in young children; and so it is a must to have syrup paracetamol at home to prevent such problems. After giving the syrup, it is better to get a paediatrician's opinion as soon as possible. Some infections causing fever can prove fatal to the child. Some fevers can become complicated and so an early diagnosis and appropriate and timely treatment is very important. So I feel that the parent should take the child to a paediatrician as soon as possible irrespective of the intensity of fever. Also remember that overdose of paracetamol is dangerous.

My son is 3 years of age. He gets fits whenever he has fever. Is he going to have fits when he grows up?

Unlikely. These fits are called 'febrile fits'. They are common among children between 6 months to 6 years of age. Give 'paracetamol' whenever he develops fever. Controlling fever is very important in preventing them from occurring. In addition, he will require another medicine to prevent the fits from occurring whenever he has fever. Talk to your paediatrician about it.

Is it necessary to heavily clothe the child if he is running a high fever?

No. just dress him to keep him comfortable. Do not overclothe him.

My son is having throat pain, cough and fever for the past 2 days. What do I do?

Consult a paediatrician. The paediatrician may prescribe your son antibiotics if he/she suspects bacterial infection of your son's throat. ***Incomplete treatment of such bacterial infections can sometimes even cause problems for the heart valves in the future. Therefore, adequate treatment of sore throat as recommended by the paediatrician is a must.*** Fever and cough can be due to infection of the sinuses, throat, airways and the lungs. A paediatrician's assessment is a must in all cases of fever with cough.

My son's tonsils are enlarged due to throat infection. Should I get them removed by operation?

Tonsils contain cells which protect your child against infection. Treating with appropriate antibiotics for appropriate period will be enough for treating the throat infection. Tonsils need to be operated and removed only if they are obstructing the child's breathing.

What diet should I give to my child after she recovers from some illness?

Your child will need more calories and protein than usual while recovering from an illness. The food needs to be easily digestible and appetising. Also ensure that good amount of fruits and vegetables are served.

What is flu?

It is an illness generally consisting of fever, cough, cold and body aches. It is caused by viruses. It is generally seasonal and spreads fast from person to person through secretions from the nose and mouth. Adequate control of fever and treatment of cold and cough is all that is needed most of the times. Rarely the infection can get serious and endanger the life of the child; especially if the child has some other underlying chronic problems like asthma, heart disease, diabetes etc. Such a child with an underlying chronic problem needs to receive 'flu' vaccines yearly starting from 6 months of age.

Should I starve my child when he has fever?

Absolutely not. In fact your child would require more calories during illness. Generally appetite would be poor during illness. So try to give easily digestible and palatable foods to the child. Do not feed him forcibly. Soups, milk, fruits, *Kichdi* etc would be good. Give him whatever he likes to eat provided they are not too oily because he may find it difficult to digest oily foods when he is ill. Avoid spicy foods because his medicines and the spices together may irritate his stomach too much and cause vomiting and stomach pain. He will need more calories and protein for around 2 weeks after he recovers from the illness. Also ensure good supply of vitamins and minerals by giving adequately balanced diet consisting of fruits and vegetables in addition to calories and protein.

My mother does not allow me to give curd and oranges to my daughter saying that she will catch cold if she eats them. Is it true?

No. In fact vitamin C present in them is supposed to boost body's immunity to some extent and help in fighting infections like common cold. Some children may be predisposed to develop cold and cough when exposed to cold foods and certain foods which do not suit them. If you have noticed that your daughter has such a tendency towards certain food items, you can consider avoiding them in her diet.

What is swine flu?

It is a type of flu with initial symptoms very similar to the seasonal flu. Swine flu can cause serious complications in vulnerable children; i.e. children less than 2 years of age and children with chronic problems like asthma, heart disease etc. Consult your doctor whenever your child develops flu like symptoms. In case fever persists for more than 3 days, or if the child develops vomiting, loose stools and decreased urine output, or if the child develops breathlessness, or if the child looks very sick and doesn't get up from the bed, or if the child does not feed well, or if the child faints, or becomes drowsy and does not respond well to you; the child needs to be taken to the doctor immediately. Medicines are available for the treatment of swine flu, but need to be used judiciously by doctors because of the side effects associated with them. It is important that vulnerable kids are treated early rather than wait for the confirmation of swine flu; for the medicines to be most effective. Confirmation of swine flu is done by taking a throat swab and identifying the virus in the lab. Vaccines for swine flu are available. Vulnerable children should receive them along with their regular flu vaccines. It is an optional vaccine for other kids.

❑❑❑

Allergy and Asthma

Allergy is body's reaction to a foreign material. It can be allergy to food, dust, pollen, insect bites etc. It can be contact allergy to certain clothes, leaves, cosmetics etc. Allergy can manifest as skin rash which is extremely itchy, wheezing (whistling sound while breathing out) and breathlessness, cough, sneezing and watering of eyes, cold, stomach pain, vomiting and loose stools depending on what the child is allergic to and how he has come in contact with it.

Allergic conditions are more common in those children whose parents also have some allergic conditions. Allergies are less common in those children who are exclusively breast fed till 6 months of age. Introduction of allergic foods like nuts, cow's milk, egg white, sea food, wheat, peanuts, soya etc only after one year of age decreases the likelihood of one developing allergies to these foods. Many kids outgrow their allergies to eggs, milk etc; but it is very rare for them to outgrow allergies to peanuts, shell fish etc.

Your ?s My Answers:

How do I protect my child from allergies?

The best way to avoid complications related to food allergies is to avoid the foods the child is allergic to. For that matter, avoiding the substance causing allergy is the best way to prevent most allergy related complications whether it is food allergy, skin allergy or any other form of allergy. Sometimes it may not be possible to completely avoid the allergen. Certain medicines are available to prevent allergies and to treat the allergic manifestations when they occur. Ointments are also available for skin allergies. Consult your doctor to get a better idea about the specific treatment for your child's allergy. Nowadays, doctors who specialise in 'allergy and immunology' are able to decrease the sensitivity of some children to certain allergies by various methods. Consulting them may be helpful when children have severe allergies.

How serious can allergies get?

Sometimes allergies can become life threatening. The child can become breathless and collapse. In case you are aware that the child is prone to have such serious attacks when exposed to certain allergens, it is imperative that you take every precaution to avoid that allergen. In case of a life threatening attack, the child needs to be administered a life saving drug known as epinephrine immediately. You must keep it handy always. It is a must that you learn about it from your doctor and be well-trained in administering it correctly at an appropriate dosage using the right technique in case of an emergency.

What is Asthma?

Asthma is a disease which causes the lower airways to go into spasm episodically, thus causing severe breathlessness. The attack may subside all by itself some times. Many a time, medicines need to be given in the form of puffs to terminate the attack. A child is more likely to develop asthma if the parents have asthma or other types of allergies. Many allergens can precipitate an attack of asthma. Keep the house free of dust, cockroaches and dust mites (by periodically dusting, washing and drying in sun all the curtains, blankets etc). Dust and keep the carpets, mattresses and pillows in the sun periodically to keep them dust mite free. This will decrease the incidence of allergies. Keeping away from flowers etc during the 'pollen season' will help in decreasing the asthmatic attacks in an asthmatic child. Fungus grows in the moist air cooler and AC pads. These need to be periodically cleaned and dried so as to prevent allergies that occur due to breathing in fungal spores. An asthma attack can also be precipitated by cold, exercise etc. There are medicines (given in the form of mouth puffs) to prevent such attacks. One can get a good idea about them by talking to the paediatrician. Asthma attacks are also precipitated by the infection of airways. Therefore appropriate and early treatment of such infections is important for prevention of severe attacks. More number of children are developing asthma and allergies nowadays because of the increasing amount of pollution. Appropriate and effective medicines to control the disease process so as to decrease the frequency and severity of attacks of asthma are available. Most of them need to be taken as mouth puffs and they hardly have any side effects. Paediatricians and other health care professionals need to educate parents about their use and allay their fears. Special devices called spacers are available for young children in order to enhance the delivery of the medicine into the airways. Parents should be well-versed with their usage in case their child has asthma.

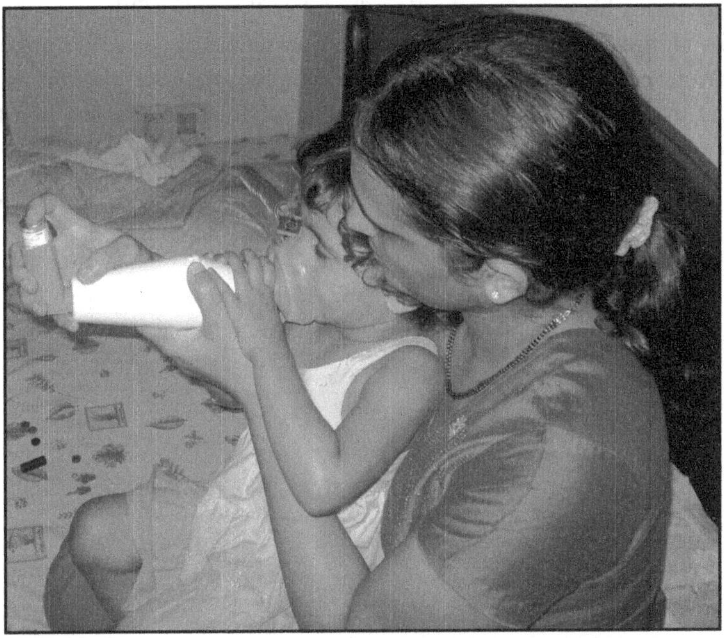

Fig: 56 Technique of using asthalin inhaler with the help of a spacer

If the child has asthma, parents should talk to the paediatrician and get a clear idea about what to do in case of an acute attack and be prepared for it at any time irrespective of whether the child is at home, school, or elsewhere. Have a look at the 'First Aid and Emergencies section'.

My son keeps coughing all the time at nights. What is the problem with him?

Infection of his sinuses (air filled gaps present in the skull around the nose) can be responsible for the cough. Asthma too may be responsible. He might be having an excess of eosinophils (a type of cells in the blood which increase in number secondary to an allergenic stimulus). Most common cause for such an increase in the number of eosinophils is the presence of worms in the gut. Consult a paediatrician and get him treated appropriately.

My child has asthma. Doctor has prescribed for my son some steroid puff to be taken every day using something called spacer. Are there any side effects with using steroids?

There are hardly any side effects with steroid puffs provided you ensure that he rinses his mouth every time he takes the puffs. Otherwise he may develop fungal infection of the mouth or hoarseness of voice. It is important for him to continue with this treatment for adequate control of his asthma. Follow the paediatrician's advice regarding when to stop giving him these puffs.

❑❑❑

Accident Prevention

Accident prevention is one of the most important aspects of child care. I have given some tips in the following pages to help you with 'accident prevention'.

Follow the given tips to safeguard your child from possible hazards:

- Keep all the medicines, kerosene, phenol, batteries etc out of reach. Let the child know a medicine as 'medicine' and not as a 'toffee' or 'sweet tonic'.
- Do not keep peanuts, button batteries or any articles of that size within the child's reach; otherwise the child may accidentally choke on them.
- Discourage children from playing and laughing with food in their mouth. Do not allow them to run around with lollipop, or other projecting objects in their mouth.
- Do not allow them to play with polythene bags; otherwise they may accidentally asphyxiate themselves (suffocate because of being unable to remove the bag from their head). Similarly, do not encourage them to hide behind curtains.
- Do not keep ropes and wires within the child's reach; otherwise they may strangulate themselves accidentally.
- Keep the bathroom doors bolted always. Keep balcony doors and gates bolted. Bolts should be out of reach of young children; otherwise they may accidentally lock themselves in, or they may open them and go outside the house without parents noticing them. Keep door stoppers in order to ensure that children do not jam their fingers in the doors.
- Ensure that child's fingers don't get jammed while closing car doors. Use seat belts while travelling in four wheelers. Use child lock for the car doors. Make sure that the child is in safe hands before you start

your vehicle; otherwise she/he may come running towards the vehicle and get injured. Do not allow children to cycle in parking lots and traffic roads. It is better to allow them to use a two wheeler in your absence only after 8 to 10 years of age. Children have to use helmets in western countries while cycling. Do not encourage children to sit on parked two wheelers.

- Always put the safety belt while using a pram, and also lock the wheels when it is not being moved around. Never leave the child alone when he/she is seated on the cot, chair etc. Avoid having chairs with wheels, rocking chairs and other easily movable furniture. Use of baby walkers should be strictly discouraged as more accidents are bound to happen with its use.
- Balcony railing should be high enough, and there shouldn't be big gaps or sharp projections. Never leave them alone on the steps. It is preferable to have a safety gate at the top and bottom of the stairs.
- Do not let children play on roof tops.
- Make an arrangement to ensure that the child doesn't roll down from the bed while asleep. Do not put the child to sleep directly under the fan or ceiling lights.
- Do not keep heavy objects on top of the shelves within children's reach; otherwise they may get injured if those objects fall on them when they try to move the objects.
- Do not leave burning objects, warmers etc in the room while the child is sleeping.
- Any spilled water or oil should immediately be mopped up.
- Carpet should not be torn or folded.
- Plug all the electric points so that children don't keep their fingers in them. No electric wires should be present within the child's reach.
- Keep all hot objects, gas and inflammable objects out of reach. Keep the child away from the kitchen, especially when you are cooking, or using grinder etc. Take care not to leave hot milk, hot oil etc within the child's reach.
- Do not leave hot iron box lying around. Avoid using table fans; otherwise children may keep their fingers inside and injure themselves.
- Sharp objects shouldn't be bought for children to play with. Keep all sharp objects like scissors, knives, forks and nails out of reach.

- Avoid using table clothes, lest the child should pull everything down from the table and injure himself/herself in the process.
- Let the furniture be such that the child cannot move under it; otherwise there is a chance that the child may bang his/her head against the furniture while standing up from beneath.
- Keep glass objects out of reach, and preferably do not have glass furniture at home. Let the furniture and window ledges etc not have sharp corners.
- Do not hold the child when sharp objects, pens, tooth picks etc are there in your hands.
- Do not leave the child alone with wax crayons in his/her hands.
- Do not let children play with stray animals like dogs.
- Never leave a young child near water in your absence, lest he/she should drown. Ensure that the swimming pools are deep enough before allowing them to dive.

Your ?s My Answers:

When can I start putting my baby in a walker?

Walkers are not to be used. Lots of accidents happen when babies are put in the walkers. Let the child learn to walk in the natural way.

What do I do if the thermometer tip breaks in the mouth accidentally?

Accidental swallowing of the mercury present at the tip of the thermometer does not cause any problem. One can safely forget about it. The vapours that come out from the spilled mercury can cause breathlessness in the short run and can affect brain, blood, kidneys and most other systems of the body in the long run. It is important that you dispose spilled mercury in a safe way. Remove all the hot objects from near the area where mercury spilled. Switch off all the fans, air conditioners etc. Open all the doors and windows. Remove all the jewels which can come in contact with mercury. Wear gloves and use a cello tape to pick up the beads of mercury. Use a torch to search for them. Do not use a broom or vacuum cleaner for cleaning up the place. Drop the beads into a plastic container and close the lid tight. Inform the 'waste collector' that the container contains hazardous waste.

❑❑❑

34

First Aid and Emergencies

This chapter is one of the most important chapters for parents wanting to give the best care to their children. All parents need to have a basic idea about first aid and basic life support measures and be prepared to tackle emergencies

Do the following if.....

- **The child suffers injury:-** If the child suffers an injury while playing, and starts to bleed from the wound, try to stop the bleeding by applying firm pressure using a clean cloth for at least 5 minutes. Wash the area with soap and clean water, and pat it dry with a clean cloth. Take him to a doctor for further management.
- **The child gets bitten by a dog:-** If the child gets bitten by a dog, clean the area with soap and water thoroughly and take him to a doctor immediately. He will require a vaccine to prevent rabies. If the child gets bitten by a snake tie a cloth above the bite in such a way that you are able to pass your fingers between the cloth and the limb. Keep loosening the cloth if the limb starts to swell up. Take him to a doctor immediately while keeping the affected limb at a slightly lower level than the rest of the body.
- **the child suffers a burn: -** If the child suffers burns, try to remove the clothing which is not sticking to his body. Remove him from the smoke so that he doesn't inhale the poisonous fumes. Wash the burnt area in clean tap water. Wrap the burnt area with a clean towel and take him to the hospital. Also remove any bracelets etc that he is wearing on the affected limb.
- **The child swallows any poisonous substance: -** If the child swallows any poisonous substance, rush her to the doctor immediately and also

carry the bottle containing the poisonous substance along with you to show to the doctor.

- **The child touches a live wire: -** If the child touches a live wire and gets electrocuted, try to dislodge him from the wire using a dry stick. Give first aid to his burns and take him to the doctor immediately.
- **The child suffers from high fever: -** If the child is suffering from very high fever, give paracetamol syrup according to the dosage written on the bottle and take her to the doctor immediately. Sponge the child using a cloth dipped in clean tap water especially on the face, trunk, under the arms and in the groin while on your way to the hospital. Do not use cold water for sponging.
- **The child develops a severe bout of asthma: -** If the child develops a severe bout of asthma at home, give her 2 asthalin puffs using a spacer and take her to the hospital if there is no improvement. Once the child is diagnosed to have asthma, you have to learn from the doctor everything about it and about the use of asthalin and spacers from the paediatrician and be prepared to manage an attack at any time. Her teachers also need to know about it. Let her carry asthalin inhaler and spacer always with her.
- **The child is diabetic: -** If the child is a diabetic, there is a chance of him developing low blood glucose due to excessive dosage of insulin. He will start being irritable, may sweat excessively, become drowsy or may even lose consciousness. Try to give him around 4 teaspoons of sugar or toffees and see if he improves. Always keep some toffees with you to give to him just in case he develops low blood glucose. Take him to the doctor after that. If he loses consciousness try to manage him like one would manage any unconscious child.
- **The child develops cramps, nausea etc: -** Many times children play in the hot sun and develop cramps, nausea, vomiting, headache etc and sometimes may even faint. In such a case take the child to a cool well-ventilated place, loosen his clothes, fan him, sponge him with cloth dipped in clean tap water(not cold water), and give him plenty of water to drink. Add a pinch of salt to each tumbler of water. If you have ORS (oral rehydration solution) sachets at home, give the child ORS to drink. I have explained about ORS more in detail in the question on home treatment for diarrhoea and vomiting. If the child vomits out the fluid, try to give it again with spoon very slowly. Take

him to a doctor if he continues vomiting. If he is unconscious, he needs to be managed as any other unconscious child.

- **The child's finger gets amputated: -** In case the child's fingers get amputated (get separated from the hand) in an accident, put them in a polythene bag. Put that bag in another polythene bag containing crushed ice and take to a surgeon; preferably paediatric surgeon or plastic surgeon immediately. Do not let the ice come in direct contact with the fingers. The surgeons will be able to attach them to the hand again in many cases. At the same time, apply a compression bandage to the bleeding hand till you reach the hospital. Hold the bleeding limb at a slightly higher level than the heart while on your way to the hospital.
- **The child gets a foreign body in the eye: -** If any foreign body gets lodged in the eye, try to remove it with a clean cotton wick only if it is somewhere under the eyelids or on the white part of the eye. Wash the eye with lots of clean tap water. If it is lodged on the pigmented part of the eye ball, do not try to manually remove it as there is chance of it getting deeper into the eye and causing more damage. If any corrosive fluid, lime etc gets into the eye, wash the eye with plenty of clean water and rush the child to the hospital.
- **The child starts bleeding from the nose: -** If any child starts bleeding from the nose apply firm pressure on the affected side of the nose with the thumb or index finger pressing the outer aspect of the nose against the central part.

  It is preferable to keep the head leaning forward so that the child doesn't swallow blood.

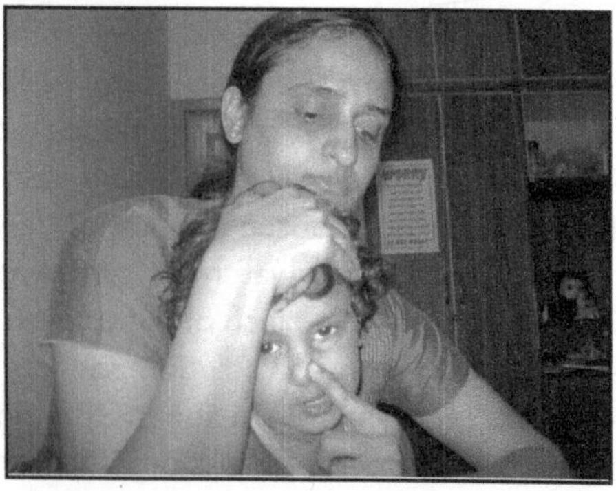

Fig: 57 Technique to control nose bleed by applying pressure

One can dip a cloth in cold water and use it to apply pressure in the same way. Take her to the doctor after that. If any foreign body gets lodged in the nose, take the child to the hospital. Do not try to remove it yourself.

- **The child looses a permanent tooth: -** If any permanent tooth comes off from the socket, put it in cold milk after washing it. Try to reach the dentist immediately so that it can be reimplanted. Milk teeth are not reimplanted; and so you need not carry them to the hospital. If the child is bleeding continuously from the gums, make him bite on a clean cold wet cloth and take him to the hospital immediately.
- **The child gets stung by honeybee: -** If the child gets stung by honeybees or wasps etc, rush him to the hospital without delay because some children can develop severe allergic reaction to the sting which can endanger the child's life.
- **The child develops skin reaction: -** If the child develops any skin reaction or breathlessness after administering a new medicine or after eating any new food item, rush him to the hospital before the allergic reaction becomes severe and endangers his life.
- **The child sustains a fracture: -** If a child sustains a fracture, that particular limb needs to be immobilised as much as possible and the child has to be taken to the hospital immediately. It is better to go through various first aid books to get an idea about various methods of immobilising the fractured limbs.
- **The child falls from a height: -** If the child falls from a height or is injured in an accident or has nearly drowned, he might have sustained a fracture; sometimes even at the neck. Try not to move him too much. Gently tap him and ask loudly if he is okay or call out his name. If he moves, cries or answers, quickly check for injuries and the need for medical assistance. If necessary and you are alone, leave him in the position in which you have found him and immediately call the emergency medical services team. If you have somebody with you, tell them to call the emergency medical services team. Go back to the child and keep monitoring him till help arrives. Ensure that he is in a safe place and that he is breathing regularly. If you have to shift him to a safe place, take care not to turn or twist his head and neck while picking him up. In case he starts gasping or stops responding to your call, call for help and then proceed with resuscitating the child.

Do the following to revive the child:

1. Ensure that the rescuer and the child are in a safe place. Ensure that he is on a flat and hard surface. Turn him over carefully to a 'face up' position. Minimise turning and twisting of the head and neck while moving him or turning him over. Taking care of his airway is the first thing that you should do. Use one hand to tilt the forehead in such a way that the neck gets slightly extended. Use the index finger and middle finger of the other hand to lift the bony part of the chin up as depicted below. Do not press on the soft tissues of the neck. Ensure that the mouth is open. Look at the chest movements, listen to his breath sounds, and feel for the air movement on your cheek and decide quickly if the child is breathing or not.

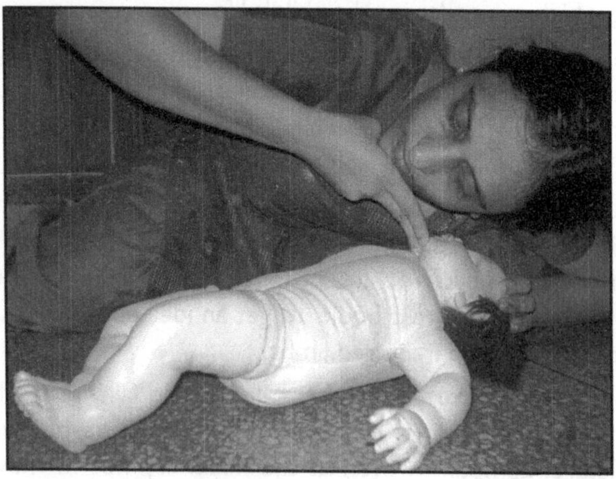

Fig: 58 Head tilt-chin lift; look, feel and hear for breathing

2. If the child is breathing regularly, put him in recovery position as shown below. The neck needs to be slightly extended (by gently tilting the head back). You can support the back with something like a pillow or a rolled up blanket. The idea is to put him in such a way that the secretions drain out from the mouth, the airway is maintained, the air way is easily observed and the movement of the head and neck is minimised.

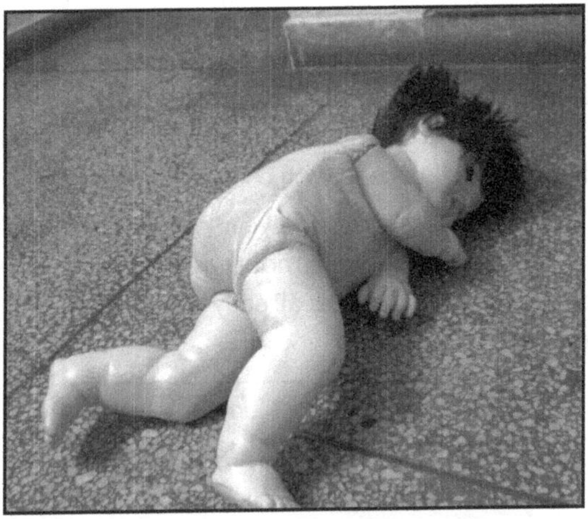

Fig: 59 Recovery position

3. If the child is not breathing or is gasping, remove any visible foreign material present in his mouth and start giving rescue breaths. Do not attempt blind finger sweep to remove a suspected foreign body that you are not able to visualise. If you attempt such a thing, you may in fact push the foreign body further down into the airway and cause complete airway obstruction. Pinch the nose (in order to close it) of the child with the index finger and thumb of the same hand that you are using to maintain the head tilt. Make a tight seal with your mouth around the child's mouth and blow in air as shown below.

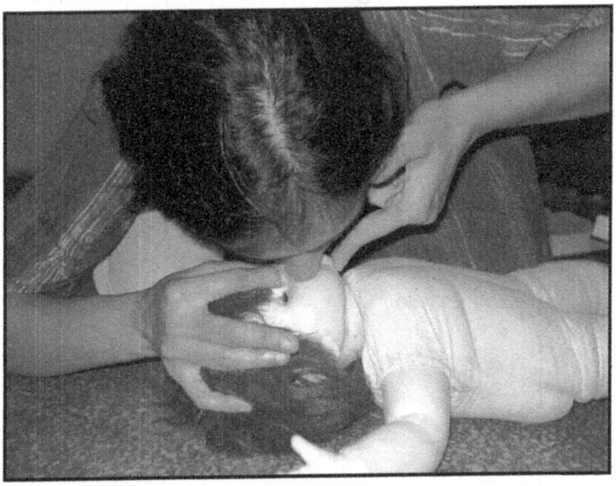

Fig: 60 Head tilt, chin lift and mouth to mouth breathing

4. If the breaths are effective, the chest wall will rise with every breath and fall when air comes out. Give each breath over a period of 1 to 1 ½ seconds. Pause after each breath to take a breath. Give 2 rescue breaths. Do not overdo the head tilt; otherwise you will be extending the neck too much. Proceed with chest compressions after two breaths.
5. In case it is a baby less than one year of age, the nose is not pinched. Instead a tight seal with your mouth is made around the mouth and nose and breaths are given as already mentioned. Index finger would suffice for lifting the chin up.

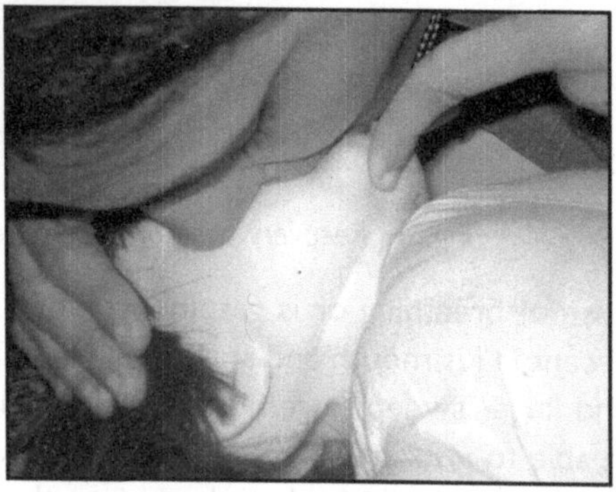

Fig: 61 Mouth-to-mouth breathing by making a tight seal around the mouth and the nose

6. In order to give chest compressions to a baby less than 1 year of age, index finger and middle finger are used to press the breast bone down to one third to one half of the total depth of the chest, just below the level of nipples . Maintain head tilt with the other hand.

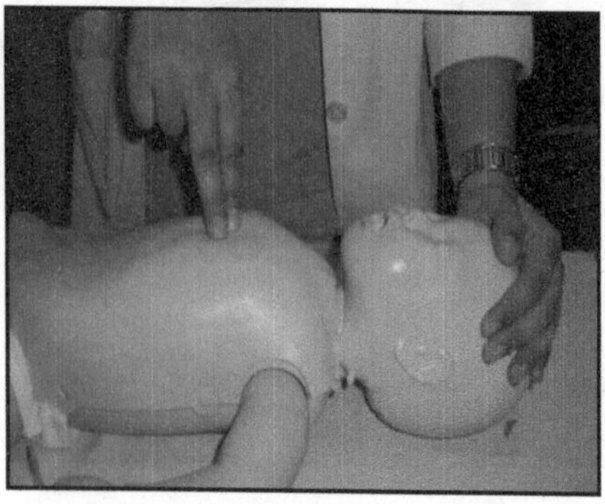

Fig: 62 Chest compressions for an infant (less than one year of age)

7. In case of older children, heel of one hand or sometimes, heels of both hands held one above the other need to be used for giving chest compressions. The compressions are given at the level of the nipples (on the lower part of the breast bone).

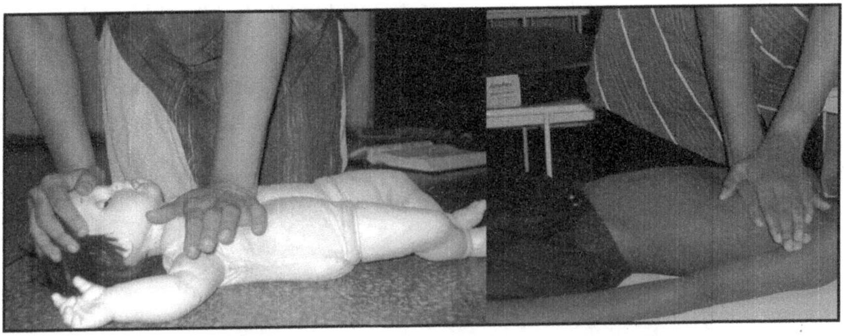

Fig: 63 Chest compressions for children more than 1 year of age

The elbow needs to be straight so that right amount of pressure gets to the heart for it to start beating. Ensure that you have compressed the breast bone to one third to one half of the total depth of the chest. 30 chest compressions need to be followed by 2 breaths if you are alone. You can use your other hand for maintaining the head tilt. If there are 2 rescuers, 15 chest compressions need to be followed by 2 breaths. The second person can maintain the airway with the head tilt- chin lift maneuver when the first person is giving the chest compressions. In a child older than 8 years, 15 compressions need to be followed by 2 breaths irrespective of the number of rescuers available. Chest compressions and artificial breathing need to be continued till the child starts breathing, or till medical help comes; whichever is earlier. If you are fatigued and not able to give compressions, let some body take over. ***Take care not to press upon the ribs or the tip of the breast bone***. Many times non medical people find it difficult to give effective rescue breaths in which case chest compressions at least have to be given. There is also the problem of infection while giving rescue breaths to an unknown child. You can use a thin cloth as a barrier between your mouth and the child's in such a case. If you are alone, continue resuscitation for at least 2 minutes (5 cycles) before trying to activate the emergency medical team. If some one else is there with you, you can ask them to activate the emergency medical team while you are resuscitating the child.

8. If a baby less than one year of age chokes on a foreign body (pea nuts etc) and ***is not able to cough effectively, or not able to cry, or is becoming limp, or is gasping and producing a high-pitched sound while breathing in***, hold him as shown below and try to expel the foreign body out. Support the head and neck by firmly holding the jaw. Do not press on the soft part of the neck while holding him; otherwise you will further obstruct his airway. Head end has to be at a lower level as shown below so that gravity aids in getting the foreign body out. Give 5 back slaps between the shoulder blades using the heel of your hand.

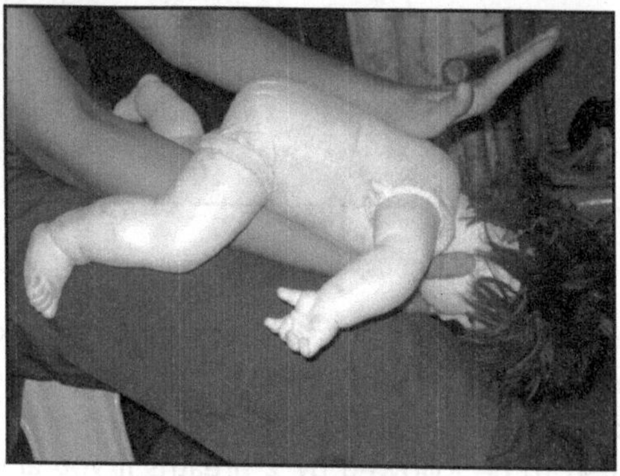

Fig: 64 Back slaps

Turn him over carefully. Keeping the head end lower than the rest of the body, use index finger and middle finger to press on the breast bone just below the level of nipples to a depth of around one third to half of the total depth of the chest. Do this five times.

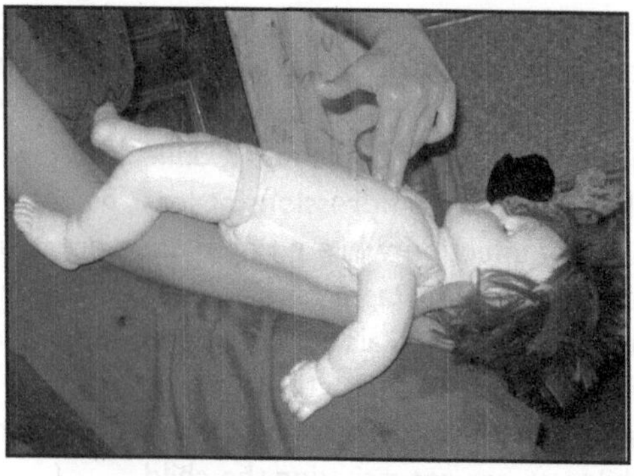

Fig: 65 Chest compressions in an infant for expelling the foreign body

Keep repeating the entire cycle of 5 back slaps and 5 chest thrusts till the foreign body comes out or till the child loses consciousness. Do the maneuvers slowly. The idea is to increase the pressure in the chest so as to expel the foreign body out. ***Do not attempt these maneuvers if the child is coughing loudly and is able to cry. Coughing is the safest and most effective way of expelling the foreign body out.*** In case the child loses consciousness or stops breathing, resuscitate him as I have elaborated above.

9. If the child is older than one year; keep him vertical, hold him from behind, fist one hand and place it between the belly button and the tip of the breast bone, fist the other hand over the first one and pull backwards and upwards (Heimlich maneuver). You can either stand or kneel down behind the child for doing this maneuver. Repeat the maneuver till the foreign body is expelled. Take care not to touch the ribs or the breast bone while doing it. Have a look at the following picture.

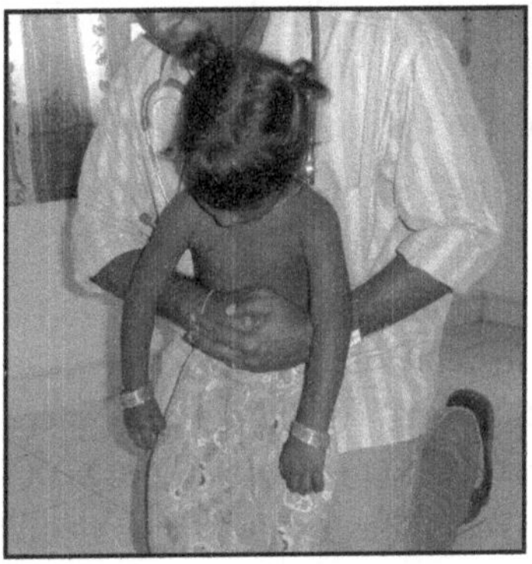

Fig: 66 Heimlich maneuver

In case the child loses consciousness or stops breathing, resuscitate him as I have elaborated above.

10. After rescuing a child from a near drowning incident, do not try to empty her stomach by pressing on it as that would cause further complications. She will need to be resuscitated if she is not breathing and is unresponsive. Have a look at what I have written about resuscitating an unconscious child. She might have sustained a neck or spine fracture. Support the body and take care not to turn and twist the head and neck if you have to move her. Foreign bodies like stones, weeds etc may be obstructing the airway. Try to look for them whenever you give rescue breaths to the child.

11. If a child throws fits and loses consciousness or loses consciousness due to any other reason, follow the same protocol that I have elaborated for managing an unconscious child.

It is better that one goes through books and videos available on these techniques of resuscitation and methods of first aid and be prepared for emergencies rather than trying to open a book to find out what to do when the emergency had already occurred. Keeping the emergency phone numbers written separately and saving them in the cell phones is very important. I have tried to cover most situations for which first aid can be given by non medical persons ; leaving out those situations where nothing much can be done except for rushing the child to the hospital.

Your ?s My Answers:

My daughter is 4 years of age. She keeps getting minor wounds while playing. How do I treat them at home? Do I have to give antibiotics to prevent infection? Do I have to give her a TT injection every time?

All that you have to do is to wash the wound with clean water and soap, pat it dry and cover it with a bandage whenever she goes out to play and when she is sleeping so that the secretions don't stick to the bed sheet. Otherwise leave the wound open for faster healing. There is absolutely no need for antibiotics unless the wound gets infected. If your daughter is appropriately vaccinated i.e. has received 3 doses of DPT in her 1st year and a booster dose at 1 ½ years of age, there is no need to give her TT after an injury. Her next vaccination is due at 5 years of age.

What should my first aid kit contain?

First aid kit at homes should contain spirit, sterile cotton, sterile gauze and band aids. It should also contain emergency drugs as per the doctor's recommendations in case the child is prone to develop some acute problems like an asthmatic attack or severe allergic reaction or fits etc. It is advisable to have paracetamol syrup also at home.

How do I take care of small wounds at home?

Wash the wound with clean water and soap. Clean the area surrounding the wound with cotton soaked in spirit. Apply band aid in such a way that some amount of air reaches the wound. This will help in quicker healing of the wound. If the wound does not heal, or if the area around the wound swells up, or if foul smelling discharge comes from it, or if the child develops fever; do consult a doctor.

What do I do for a thorn prick?

Press firmly the surrounding area to expel the thorn out. Apply pressure to stop bleeding. Clean the area thoroughly with soap and water. Apply cold compress to the surrounding area for relief of pain. It is important to ensure that your child had received his Tetanus shots as per schedule; otherwise he may require a Tetanus shot now. Consult a doctor and ensure complete removal of the thorn. In case the same situation arises with a glass piece, it is better to take the child to the hospital unless one is very sure that the glass has not got stuck in the flesh. Firm pressure to stop bleeding is a must. In case pain persists, or the area swells up, or if the child develops fever, or if foul smelling discharge comes from the wound, or if the child has not received his Tetanus shots as per schedule; do consult a doctor.

❑❑❑

35

Behaviour, Discipline, Habits and Psychologic Problems

There are various factors which influence how a child is going to behave. With a little bit of common sense and a little more of patience, parents can bring their children up in a good way. **Follow the given tips to help your child grow happy and healthy:**

- **Respect the individuality of the child:-** Firstly, parents should understand that each child has a personality of his/her own. The individuality of the child needs to be respected, rather than expecting the child to behave in a perfect manner.
- **Understand your child:-** It's important for the parents to understand the developmental stage of the child and handle the child accordingly. For example, if a girl 2 years of age throws food all over the place while eating, there is no point in trying to explain to her about table manners etc. Instead, let her enjoy her meal and be happy that she is not fussing about eating food.
- **Make the child feel secure:-** Ensure that the child feels secure by showing the child your love for him/her in various ways. Spend adequate time with the child and enjoy this time, rather than counting the number of hours you are spending with the child. Most childhood behavioural problems arise out of insecurity. This needs to be kept in mind when you are tackling problems like jealousy, stealing, lying, shyness etc.
- **Set a good example:-** Practise what you preach and be a good example to the child.
- **Discipline them at the right time:-** Start disciplining the child somewhere around 3 years of age when the level of understanding of

the child is up to it. Prior to that, it is important for you to know that kids tend to do exactly opposite of what you want them to do. They try to assert their independence. So, stopping them for every small thing will only add to your irritation because they are anyway not going to oblige. The only way to handle kids at this age is to allow them to mess around a little bit as long as it is not going to harm them in anyway. At the same time, be consistent and firm in dealing with tantrums. For example if your 2 year old son is throwing a tantrum because you didn't give him a toffee, just pick him up, hug him and divert his attention. Giving him a toffee will only reinforce his behaviour. At the same time, allowing him to go on crying will make him feel insecure.

- **Maintain consistency:-** Be consistent in what you teach, and do not confuse the child by constantly changing your approach towards the child's behaviour. Similarly, both parents should teach the child similar type of behaviour and should not confuse the child by teaching contradicting things.
- **Spend quality time:-** Try to spend quality time with the child. Be a child, when you are with the child. Do not be a boring and impatient parent. Encouragement and appreciation of the child's newly acquired skills and imagination is important.
- **Stop being overprotective:-** Do not be overprotective and overanxious. Allow the child certain amount of independence, keeping a watchful eye on the child at the same time.
- **Stop being critical:-** You should neither be too strict and critical, nor be too indulgent. Your criticism of the child should be constructive. Never erode the child's confidence. Also do not teach the child to be too docile.
- **Do not bribe to make him do things:-** Never bribe the child to make him/her eat food, to make him/her listen to you, otherwise this habit will persist even when the child grows older.
- **Be careful with punishments:-** Punishment can be in the form of showing your displeasure and not responding to the child's overtures for some time depending on the age of the child. That will make the child understand that he/she has done something wrong. Try not to punish or reprimand the child for insignificant things so that the child understands it when he/she has done something really wrong. Avoid beating the child. Do not insult children in front of others for their

mistakes. Encourage children to correct their mistakes by hugging and kissing them and praising them whenever they make an effort to correct themselves. The child should never feel so scared of you that he/she will lie to you about anything.

- **Respect the child's moods:-** Remember that your child is not a puppet who will keep telling rhymes and dancing to songs whenever you want. Respect the child's moods.
- **Avoid doing certain things:-** Do not discuss the child in his presence.

  Avoid arguing and fighting in front of the child.

  Do not show favouritism.
- **Stop putting unnecessary pressures:-** Forcing a child every time to do what he/she doesn't want to do will make the child rebellious. The child will develop aversion towards that act. For example, if you keep forcing food into the mouth of your one-and-half-year old daughter, she will only refuse it more and more and will loose appetite for food in the long run.
- **Instill good values:-** Teach children to say 'sorry' and 'thank you' from as early as 1 ½ to 2 years of age. Teach them to share their toys with other kids.
- **Be strict at times:-** Do not give in to their every demand. Let them understand that not all of their demands will be met with.
- **Give them freedom of expression but in the right way:-** Allow the children to express themselves. Teach them to express their feelings in words rather than undesirable actions. For example if a four year old boy starts hitting at his mother because she didn't buy him a football, he should be taught to express the same feeling of anger by saying "Mom, I'm angry with you because you didn't buy me a football." Gradually, he will learn to say that rather than hitting at his mother.
- **Try to take a deep insight into their insecurities:-** Various habits like nail biting, hair plucking, tics (repeated blinking, wincing etc) head banging, etc arise out of insecurity. Children do it more to get attention. Ignore them, and try to address the underlying insecurity and anxiety. This is the best way to get the child rid of those habits.
- **Take care of their diet and sleep:-** Hunger, tiredness and sleepiness etc lowers the child's threshold to irritant stimuli and will increase the

behavioural problems. Ensure that the child sleeps and eats well.

- **Be firm:-** Curtail your child's aggressive behaviour from the very beginning, especially if he shows tendency towards destroying objects, harming insects, birds etc and hitting others. Firmness is necessary in dealing with such behaviours.

Family plays the most important role in ensuring that a child grows up to be a confident, compassionate and well-behaved child with good values. Domestic violence, parental inconsistency, stressors like loss of a loved one, change of place, hospital admission etc; excessive stress placed on the child at school, bullying at school etc can be responsible for various psychological problems like excessive anxiety, depression, irritability, phobias, body aches, headache, stomach pain etc. For children with chronic problems like asthma, joint pains etc stress can worsen their problem. Whenever it looks like your child is having some behavioural problem or alteration in mood etc, do consult a paediatrician. After appropriate evaluation, the paediatrician would refer the child to a psychiatrist if necessary. Parents should not hesitate to meet a child psychiatrist if necessary. Parents should not be under the impression that their child was referred to a psychiatrist because he/she has some serious mental ailment. They should understand that expert management of psychological problems is very important in helping the child to overcome his/her problem.

Some times the problem may be very severe. A child may be displaying multiple problems like aggression, disruptive behaviour, stealing, lying, cruelty to animals, swearing, throwing tantrums all the time etc.

- A child may be having compulsions like ritual hand washing, touching certain objects, checking doors etc.
- Some children may develop severe phobia towards social settings (including school, family get-togethers etc).
- Some children may develop unrealistic worries about separation from their parents and have frequent night mares about the same.
- Some children tend to have stereotypical behaviour, poor eye contact, poor speech, poor interaction with others, tend to dislike even the slightest change in their routine and surroundings, and prefer solitary play. This disorder in children is known as ***autistic disorder***; and develops before 3 years of age.

These children need to be treated by using various approaches. Family plays a very important role in treating these children. Medicines may also be needed in addition to other approaches. Parents need to seek expert help at the earliest. The earlier we intervene the better the chance that the child will grow up to live a near normal life.

Your ?s My Answers:

My son is 3 years of age. He keeps throwing tantrums. How do I handle him?

Tantrums are normal at this age. Start by being very firm in not giving in to his unreasonable demands. If you reinforce his behaviour by giving in to his unreasonable demands he is going to continue to throw more tantrums to get whatever he wants. Instead try to divert him with something more interesting or just ignore his behaviour till he calms down. Try to pick him up and comfort him, but do not give in to his demands. At the same time do not beat or punish him. Punishing him or shouting at him will make him more stubborn. Talk to him and explain to him in a way he can understand once he calms down and is in a more receptive mood.

My elder son is 4 years of age. My younger son is 2 months of age. The elder one keeps trying to pinch the younger one. He seems to resent his presence. What can I do to tackle this problem?

Firstly, try to make him feel responsible for his baby brother. Allow him to apply oil, or tell him to sit and guard him, or allow him to arrange the baby's cupboard.

Your presence is also needed at the same time. Never leave the baby alone with the elder one. Try to give your elder son more attention than what you might be giving now so as to decrease his insecurity. Give him more hugs and kisses. Show him your appreciation whenever he displays his love towards his younger brother. Do not keep shouting whenever he comes near the baby. Let him touch and play with his younger brother, of course in your presence. Teach him to be gentle. With time he will learn to feel responsible for his baby brother and start loving him rather than competing with him.

My daughter is 2 years of age. She continues to suck her thumb even during the day time. How do I get her to get rid of this habit? I am worried that she may develop buck teeth.

Many kids develop this habit between 3 to 6 months of age. They suck their fingers either when they are hungry, or to satisfy their urge to suck, or to explore their bodies, or to feel secure. Many of them outgrow the habit by themselves. Allow your child to outgrow the habit herself. Do not scold her, or ridicule her for it. Provide a secure environment at home. Keep her engaged in various activities. Distract her whenever she tries to suck her thumb. Make her feel comfortable at bed time. Allow her to comfort herself to sleep by hugging her favourite doll. Reward her and praise her when she makes an attempt to resist herself from sucking her thumb. Milk teeth are lost and eruption of permanent teeth starts from 6 years of age. This habit will not cause her to develop buck teeth unless it persists till 6 years of age when permanent teeth start erupting.

My son is 5 years of age. Of late he is complaining of body aches almost every day. The paediatrician says that he does not need any medicine. What do I do?

Your son is most probably facing some kind of stress at school or at home. Try to identify the stressor and tackle the problem accordingly.

My son is 2 years of age. Of late, he has started to stop breathing and some times becomes blue and faints. This invariably happens whenever we do not give in to his demands or scold him. The paediatrician told us that he needs no treatment. How do we tackle the issue?

These spells that your son is having are known as 'breath-holding spells'. The only way to tackle them is by placing him safely in bed and by refusing to pamper him for a given period of time until he recovers completely. Pampering him and fussing about these spells would reinforce his behaviour. Once he understands that he is not going to get any extra attention from you, he will gradually stop holding his breath whenever he is upset and the frequency of these spells will come down. These spells do not persist beyond 5 years of age. ***Parents should never self diagnose such conditions. A paediatric consultation is a must for the diagnosis.***

❑❑❑

36

Child Care Centre, School and Learning Problems

With many women working in the offices nowadays and many families being nuclear families, there is an increasing need for child care centres.

Follow the given tips to choose a good centre for your child if the need arises:

- Choose a centre close to your work place so that you can drop in any time.
- Choose a centre where there is a favourable child: care taker ratio; say around 5 to 6: I for grown up children and 2 to 4:I for younger children and babies. The lesser the ratio, the better.
- The rooms need to be spacious, colourful, stimulating, and well-ventilated. It is preferable to go for a centre with a good open area for kids to play. It is more preferable if the centre has slide, see saw, swing etc in the open area.
- Utmost importance is to be given for hygiene. The kitchen and toilets should be maintained in a hygienic manner. It is preferable to have separate potties for toddlers. Disposable tissues should be used for cleaning the nose etc. strict hand washing practices are a must. Foot wear from outside should not be brought into the rooms. There should be separate foot wear for every one for using inside the rooms. Children with fever, cough, cold, loose stools etc should be not allowed till they recover from their illness; lest the infection should spread to other children. The centre should be kept free from mosquitoes, flies and other insects and pests. Safe drinking water should be available round the clock. Facilities for safe storage of food should be present.

- It is preferable if the care centre has a good transport facility. Young kids should never be allowed to sit on their own in the bus/ van. They have to be held by an adult.
- The care takers and teachers should have a pleasant personality. They should be patient and enjoy their job. They should be the type of people who will stimulate the child in such a way that the best is brought out from him/her.

Your ?s My Answers:

When can I put my baby girl in a care centre?

I cannot give you a fixed answer for that. It depends on when you have to join work, whether yours is a nuclear family or joint family etc. You have to plan it well ahead and prepare yourself and the baby for the same. For example if you want to send the baby to a baby care centre when she is 5 months of age, practise expressing , storing and feeding her breast milk from at least 15 days before. I would prefer that you delay sending your baby to baby care centre at least till she is toilet trained, and she is able to tell you to some extent about her day in the centre.

How do I choose a school for my son?

Many tips that I have given you for choosing a child care centre hold good for choosing his school too. The school should be such that teachers do not give corporal punishment, or do not insult the child. The schools should lay emphasis on the overall development of the child. The teachers should encourage and appreciate the talents of the child. Emphasis should be laid on learning of mother tongue. There should not be any ranking system. Undue stress regarding exams should not be placed on kids. Too much home work and too heavy bags should be a taboo.

What is the right age for me to put my daughter in school?

Nowadays informal schooling starts in many places at the age of 2 years. I would advise you to wait till at least 2½ to 3 years of age. By then most kids would be toilet trained. They will start enjoying the company of other kids. You can send her to a play school at that age. Formal schooling can start when the child is 4 years of age.

My son is 5 years of age. He is just not able to sit at one place. The teachers complain that he has very poor concentration. He is not performing well at school.

Firstly, stop nagging him about his performance at school. Request his teachers not to nag him too. Give him tasks like making a home with building blocks, making toys with modelling clay, drawing, solving puzzles etc which would require his concentration. Gradual improvement in his concentration would occur. Make learning enjoyable. Teach him about trees, flowers, colours etc when you take him out for a walk. Play word games with him. Do not put undue stress on him regarding exams. Encourage his other skills and talents. Allow adequate time for play. Give him confidence. His fidgetiness will decrease gradually and his grades will improve. In case his lack of attention, his fidgetiness and poor school performance do not improve, you should consult a child psychiatrist.

My 5-year-old son hates going to school. What do I do?

Go to his school and try to find out if the atmosphere at school is right for your child or not? Talk to him and try to find out why he does not want to go to school? The teacher may be treating him badly, or the seniors may be bullying him. Tackle the problem accordingly. Address his fears and anxiety with utmost care and gentleness.

Should I send my son for tuition?

If you have put him in a good school and you are capable of helping him with his studies, there is no need for tuition. In case you are not good with some subjects, you can let him be tutored by some one else. Do not make him spend the entire evening with books. Allow him good amount of play time.

My daughter has problem with reading books. Her IQ otherwise appears to be okay. What should I do?

This kind of reading disability is known as ***dyslexia***. Your daughter needs help from experts who treat such children. You too will need to play an important role in helping her over come her problem. Do consult a paediatrician who would guide you appropriately.

❑❑❑

Adoption

Adopting a child has many angles to it. There is an emotional angle, social angle and very importantly a legal angle.

Following are some tips which may help you before you go in for an adoption:

- Be sure about adopting a child. Be sure that the entire family is ready for it so that the child doesn't face any rejection from them in the future.
- Meet the right people in orphanages and ensure that the legal process of adoption is adhered to.
- Obtain detailed history about the biological parents and their family. Be sure that there is no inheritable disease running in the family. Let a paediatrician assess the child thoroughly, If need be, some investigations may have to be carried out to be sure that the child is not harbouring any serious infection/ illness. This process is simpler if you are adopting somebody from within the family; but emotional and legal problems may occur later on if the biological parents want the child back.
- Try to adopt the child at a younger age so that a better bond forms between the child and the adopted parents.
- Be open with the child about the adoption. You can start telling the child about it as early as 3 to 4 years taking into consideration the child's level of understanding.
- Do not allow relatives to show their rejection towards the child. It is better to keep the child away from such relatives.

❑❑❑

Child Abuse

Child abuse existed for ages, but is being increasingly recognized of late. Child abuse can be physical or psychological. Physical abuse can range from depriving the child of food, clothes, home, education, treatment of ailments and safety to inflicting injuries and abusing the child sexually. Psychological abuse can range from depriving the child of love, encouragement, support and stimulation to terrorizing and insulting the child.

All these forms of abuse will have an adverse impact on the child's physical and psychological development. The child can be abused by relatives, friends, care takers, teachers and many other people. Parents need to be alert to changes in the behavior of their child and signs of abuse so as to protect their child from further abuse. The child may refuse to be left alone with that particular person, or may refuse to go to school, or may even start talking about some body touching his/her genitalia etc. Be alert and protect your child from abuse before it is too late.

❑❑❑

Miscellaneous

My son is 6 years of age. He has small round swellings on both sides of his neck. What are they?

They are 'lymph nodes'. They produce cells and substances to fight infections. They are present in many places in the body. A paediatrician needs to be consulted if they are unduly enlarged.

Can I give honey to my son 8 months of age?

Certain microorganisms which can grow in improperly preserved honey produce toxic substances which when ingested can cause paralysis (inability to use hands, legs etc.). This is more common with infants (children less than 1 year of age). So it is better to avoid honey till at least one year of age.

How do I administer medicines to my child?

Most medicines for children are available in liquid form. You can give them using a spoon. Give medicines when the child is sitting. Never give medicines when the child is lying down. Measure the exact dose using the marked cup/dropper that the manufacturer supplies along with the medicine. ***Do not try to give tablets or capsules to a child till he/she is at least 5 years of age, and is willing to take the medicine. Forcing the child to take tablets may result in the child choking on the tablets.*** If the need arises that the child has to take a tablet, then crush it and mix it with some water or sauce and administer it in the liquid form. Dispersible tablets are also available for many medicines. These dissolve very easily in water. Try to administer medicines to the child by diverting them towards something else so that they do not have enough time to realise that they are being given some medicine. This will save you the trouble of administering medicine to a protesting child. Administering medicine to a protesting child can result in the child choking on the medicine.

Fig: 67 Administering medicine to a toddler

My son is 4 years of age. He is left handed. He uses his left hand even for eating food. How do I change his handedness?

Forcibly trying to change him will adversely affect his skills and talents and will put lot of pressure on him. Let him be a left handed person. Do not try to change it. More important than teaching him to eat with right hand is to teach him to wash his hands with soap and water before eating food and whenever he uses the toilet.

What precautions should I take when my son insists on playing in the hot sun?

Try to discourage him from playing in the sun as much as possible if it is very hot outside. Tell him to take sips of water in between if he insists on playing in the sun. You can add some salt to his drinking water. Make him wear light-coloured cotton clothes. If his skin is sensitive to sun, you may have to start using a sunscreen of SPF (skin protection factor) 15 to 20. Choose those sunscreens which do not become messy once he starts sweating. Some children may need sunscreens of higher SPF. It is better to talk to a skin specialist in such a case. Tell him to return home if he develops headache, dizziness, cramping pain in the legs etc. In such a case, treat him at home by making him lie down in a cool well-ventilated place. Fan him, give him plenty of water with a little amount of salt added to it, and sponge him with a cloth dipped in clean tap water (do not use cold water).

My son is 5 years of age. Why does he complain of headache always?

Try to see if he is tense about something; and if so relieve his anxiety. Make sure he has regular eating habits and doesn't remain hungry half the time. Ensure that he drinks adequate water. Excess heat can precipitate a head ache; and so discourage him from playing in the hot sun. Get his eyes checked once. Infection of sinuses (air filled gaps present in the skull around the nose) is also an important cause for headache. Therefore an ENT consultation may be needed. If the headache is severe, or if he is waking up every morning with a headache, or if he vomits every time he has a headache; consult a paediatrician immediately.

How do I care for my child's feet?

Good foot wear which does not result in overcrowding of the toes is a must. Keep the feet clean and dry to prevent fungal infections. Apply good amount of cream to the heel and sole to prevent cracking.

My son keeps vomiting when he travels by bus. What do I do?

Talk to your doctor and give him the medicine that he/she prescribes around 30 minutes before the journey. The medicine may even make your son sleepy. Do not give any oily or spicy food just before the journey. Do not talk about his vomiting in front of him. Divert his attention completely during the journey. Do not make him sit on those seats which are just above the wheels. Avoid travelling when it is very hot. Carry disposable bags with you just in case he decides to vomit. Also carry ORS (oral rehydration solution) sachets and water with you. You can also prepare ORS solution at home and take with you (to be discarded after 24 hours). Give ORS sip by sip. Do not allow him to gulp it down.

I have a 2-year-old daughter. Her tummy protrudes out. What can be the problem?

Protruding tummy is a common thing with all toddlers at this age. You can meet a paediatrician if it is worrying you too much.

Tell me something about jaundice.

Jaundice is due to increase of something called 'bilirubin'in the blood. It can be due to a problem with the liver. It can also be due to various other causes.The common type of jaundice is one which occurs due to infection of the liver by viruses which spread via food and water. There is no medicine for such types of jaundice. Avoid taking native medicines, as some may even worsen the problem. Give good nutrition to the child (good amounts of cereals, only moderate amounts of proteinaceous foods and very less of oily foods). Discuss with the paediatrician in detail about the diet of the child. If the child shows signs of worsening liver function like excessive sleepiness, talking incoherently etc, you will have to take the child to the paediatrician at once.

Should I use sun glasses for my child?

Yes, especially if you are going to take him out in bright sun to places like beaches, snow fields etc. Ultra violet rays and other high energy rays can cause long term problems to the eyes. Buy the sun glasses from a reputed dealer and ensure that the glasses provide 100% protection from the harmful rays. Use cords to tie the glasses to your child's head so that they do not fall off.

My daughter is 2 years of age. She has knock knees. What should I do?

Minor degrees of knock knees are common at the age of 2 to 3 years. They tend to disappear by 5 to 6 years of age. It is better to meet an orthopedician/paediatrician and get his/her opinion because rickets (due to vitamin D deficiency) and certain other conditions can also produce knock knees.

My son has flat feet. He is 3 years of age. What do I do about it?

It may get corrected as your son grows up. Many kids of his age will have the same problem. Do not worry as long as he is not affected by it. Good foot wear with a slight heel is important. If it persists and is causing him discomfort, do talk to an orthopedician.

❏❏❏

Pregnancy Care

Dr V.P. Jyotsna, MD
(Obs. & Gynae.)

I have been married for some time now and would like to plan a pregnancy. What precautions or advice is needed?

Ideally, every couple who plans for a pregnancy must see a doctor before the pregnancy actually occurs so that they may receive advice regarding what to expect in a pregnancy and whether or not the woman is healthy enough to go through the pregnancy. It has been seen that in some women certain conditions like heart disease were detected for the first time in pregnancy. It gives an opportunity to correct any nutritional deficiencies like anaemia, and also start folate, which is nothing but one of the B-complex vitamins which is needed for proper development of the baby's nervous system.

Also it gives an opportunity to discuss diet, exercise and travel issues with regard to the pregnancy.

I was told that I can have my first check-up after 5 months? When should I see a doctor for the first time in pregnancy?

In the event that pregnancy has already occurred please see a qualified doctor as soon as the pregnancy is suspected, i.e. after a missed period. A pregnancy can usually be confirmed using any of the home based kits available in medical stores (eg: Velocit, pregcard, pregtest etc.). But in order to check that the pregnancy is normal, viable and within the uterus (womb) only and not elsewhere (ectopic pregnancy) and also to confirm the duration of pregnancy you must visit a doctor. For accurate dating of the pregnancy and also to look for any other problems in the uterus and ovaries the doctor might advise for an ultrasound examination or what we simply refer to as "scan". The doctor will also examine for any other health problems that you might incidentally have.

Why should I have these antenatal check-ups? And how often should I come to the hospital?

It is agreed that pregnancy is a normal physiological condition and not a disease but things can and do go wrong for some women. And it is not easy to predict who might have problems. There can be problems with growth of the baby, position of the baby, problems with the mother like high blood pressure, diabetes etc. which cannot be detected and treated unless and until every pregnant woman has serial antenatal (meaning "before delivery") check-ups. It also gives the doctor an opportunity to look for any minor ailments and anaemia which can be treated in the course of pregnancy. Antenatal visits are also the chance for a doctor to prepare and counsel a mother-to-be for labour, delivery and newborn care.

It is a standard recommendation that all women with uncomplicated pregnancies must have a monthly check-up until completion of 7 months or 28 weeks. From the 29th week to 36 weeks or in other words till just after the beginning of the 9th month every pregnant woman must have a check-up every 15 days. In the last month the visits to the doctor must be every week as labour might start any day and hitherto unforeseen problems might surface in the last month of pregnancy.

I have a lot of vomiting and I wish I could take something for it but my mother says I should not use any medicines in pregnancy.

Vomiting or sometimes just nausea is very common in the first 3 months of pregnancy. It is treatable and medications which have been proven to be safe are available. But please consult a doctor for the prescription. It is true that one should avoid medications in pregnancy but a doctor will advise you correctly regarding which medication is safe and which should be avoided. In any event if vomiting persists beyond the 5th month or if it is too severe, there might be other medical conditions that need to be looked for so please ask your doctor.

Can I travel during pregnancy?

Travel by a healthy woman has no harmful effect on pregnancy. Hence if your pregnancy is uncomplicated travel by trains or properly pressurised aircrafts is allowed until the last month of pregnancy. Prolonged travel wherein health facilities are not available in case a complication arises should be avoided and avoid any mode of travel which is jerky for e.g. bus or two wheeler travel on bad roads etc. You should try and walk about a little every 2 hours while travelling by train or airplane taking enough care not to lose balance or have an injury. In case the pregnancy develops any complications one should always consult their doctor before planning travel and take advice regarding any precautions. Travel by car is safe and the use of safety seat belt is not harmful to the baby. The lap belt portion of the safety harness should be placed below the abdomen and across the thighs and the shoulder belt across the chest.

Can I exercise during pregnancy?

Mild to moderate exercise can be continued during pregnancy on a regular basis up to 3 times a week provided your pregnancy is uncomplicated. Avoid vigorous exercise and any form of exercise which might need lying down or might cause loss of balance. Walking, cycling, swimming etc are good forms of exercise for pregnant women. Stop exercising when tired and avoid exhaustion. Some complications in pregnancy might benefit from rest, so if your doctor advises rests do not continue with the exercise. Yoga can be practised in pregnancy but by taking care not to put any compression on the pregnant uterus and avoiding those *asanas* which may compromise balance.

What are the dietary recommendations during pregnancy and lactation?

It is recommended that a pregnant woman must increase her daily caloric intake by 300Kcal in addition to her usual recommended intake according to weight. An average Indian woman requires about 2000-2200 Kcal per day. In the same way the Caloric intake should be increased by 550 Kcal during the post delivery lactation (breast-feeding) period. Your doctor or a nutritionist could help in planning a diet. In general,

- You can eat any safely cooked food in amounts you desire and salt to taste.
- Make sure there is ample food to eat (especially for women with nutritional deficiencies)
- Discuss your diet with your doctor occasionally.
- Take enough protein and carbohydrates and avoid excess fat in the diet. Add a fruit to the daily diet.
- Take the recommended nutritional supplements.
- Never take too many vitamin pills etc without a doctor's advice.
- Take adequate water (4-6litres) in order to avoid dehydration and constipation.

- Where pregnancy is complicated take advice regarding dietary modifications.

Can I continue to work during pregnancy?

Any job that involves severe physical strain must be avoided in pregnancy. But otherwise a woman with an uncomplicated pregnancy may continue to work till the 9th month of pregnancy, sometimes even up to the onset of labour. Any job that requires standing in the same position for long periods might predispose to preterm labour, so women in such jobs must include a routine wherein intermittent walking or sitting in a chair is possible.

Women in jobs that require continuous sitting like software professionals, clerks, tailors etc must get up and walk around every two hours. Such women are prone to back aches and may derive some benefit from using a small cushion to support the lower back.

What is Ultrasound scan for?

Ultrasonography or commonly what is referred to as "USG/ Scan" is a method to view the internal parts of the body and it uses sound waves and their reflection. It is useful when we need to image the uterus and the fetus (baby) within. It is a safe method of imaging unlike X-rays or CT-scan which can harm the fetus. In the early months the USG examination provides information about the position of the pregnancy i.e. inside the uterus, normally or in any abnormal site- ectopic. It is used to check whether the pregnancy is viable , whether the heart beat is visible, whether there is any bleeding or blood clot, whether the cervix is long enough and is closed or not. The 'cervix 'refers to the lower portion of the uterus (womb) which should be closed at all times and sufficient in length to avoid abortions or preterm labour (labour much before the expected date of delivery).

Later than 4 months the USG is generally used to look for the well-being of the fetus and whether the major organs of the body are formed well, whether there is sufficient fluid around the fetus, whether the placenta position is normal or not etc. There are many more details which are visible on an ultrasound scan depending on the complications during the pregnancy. Generally, most obstetricians advise 3-4 scans during pregnancy and they are not harmful to the fetus. Determining the sex of the fetus by an ultrasound is a punishable offence as per Indian Law (PNDT Act), hence please do not ask any sonologist or doctor performing the scan to reveal the sex of the fetus.

What is a TT shot?

TT refers to "Tetanus Toxoid" which is an injection given to provide immunity to the pregnant woman and her child against a deadly disease known as Tetanus. 2 doses of this injection in the 5th and 7th month are routinely advised.

What medicines should be used in pregnancy?

Use of medicines or drugs in pregnancy is restricted to a small number of safe drugs. So before taking any medication kindly seek the advice of your doctor. Routinely every pregnant woman is advised to take Iron, folic acid and Calcium preparations in pregnancy from the 5th month onwards. In women who are anaemic higher doses of Iron tablets or injections may be advised by the doctor. In the absence of any other complications, these medicines are sufficient. But if some complications arise, additional medications like Insulin for diabetes, drugs to reduce BP in hypertensive (high blood pressure) women may be prescribed. Any medication prescribed by the doctor will be assessed for its safety in pregnancy and then advised. Hence one should not disregard the doctors' advice and stop medications by themselves.

Why should I have all these blood and urine tests?

Every pregnant woman is screened for common medical conditions which may lead to complications during pregnancy or delivery. In order to do so a set of prescribed blood and urine tests are done routinely to check for conditions such as anaemia, diabetes, hepatitis B, exposure to syphilis, HIV status, urinary tract infection etc. If any of the reports are abnormal the doctor may advise further tests. But as a routine the above mentioned screening tests are to be done at least once and a urine examination is advised in every visit.

What is done in a routine antenatal check? How should I be prepared for it?

Every antenatal visit to the doctor comprises of a series of questions by the doctor regarding your date of the last menses (periods) and a detailed history of your health (in the first visit usually), and an enquiry of your diet and personal habits. A checking of the height & weight, blood pressure, pulse rate, and a detailed clinical examination by the doctor for the status of your pregnancy and any other medical illnesses. So before you go to visit the doctor keep all information regarding the regularity of your menses, the last date of the period, any other medical illnesses in you or your family like diabetes, hypertension, asthma, exposure to tuberculosis (TB), seizures (fits) etc. The doctor may also enquire regarding the occurrence of twins or mentally challenged children in any of the family members. Carry all reports of previous medical problems for which you might have been treated and reports of any tests that have been done recently. Details of the previous pregnancy and delivery (if any) are very important to anticipate any complications this time and to plan this delivery, so remember to carry the discharge card/ papers related to previous pregnancies.

Any kind of loose clothing is advised when you go for an antenatal visit for e.g. a sari or a salwar kurta. Ensure you carry water and something to eat while waiting for your turn in the clinic. In case you have some severe pain or bleeding or watery discharge from the vagina, please inform the nurse beforehand so that your check up is hastened.

When can I know whether I will have a normal delivery or not?

In the 9th month of pregnancy, the doctor will examine and may also ask for an ultrasound scan. Based upon the position, amount of fluid around the baby, the size of the baby and the size of the birth passage (pelvis) and the presence of any other complications in pregnancy, the attending doctor will let you know about the mode of delivery planned. In most cases a normal vaginal delivery is possible. Rarely in the presence of complications before labour starts or if complications arise during labour, a caesarean section is advised.

It's my first pregnancy how will I know when labour starts?

Labour pains usually start in the 9th month of pregnancy, and rarely before that. In most women they start with back ache and a sticky vaginal discharge which may be mixed with some blood. This is called "show". Hours later uterine contractions may start and cause abdominal pain. The labour pains are typically intermittent ("on and off") at regular intervals. As time passes they become more severe and closely spaced. Once the frequency of pains rises to once in 15-20 minutes you may start off to the hospital. In the event that pains are not increasing you are still advised to go to the hospital if there is any bleeding or watery discharge from the vagina or if the baby's movements are diminished.

What is "False labour"?

Sometimes a woman in the 9th month of pregnancy might experience back ache with mild pains on and off without actual opening up of the uterus or what is referred to as dilatation of the cervix. It is just a sign of uterine preparedness for labour without the actual onset of labour. The feeling might pass off after a few hours and some sedation. This is referred to as "false labour". It is nothing to worry about; but in order to know whether labour has set in or not the woman must be examined by a doctor. This can occur in any pregnancy but more often in the first pregnancy.

What is 'expected date of delivery'?

EDD or expected date of delivery is a date which corresponds to 40 weeks of pregnancy from the last menstrual period. It is calculated as the date 9 months from the last menstrual period plus 7 days provided the periods or menses are regular and once in 28 days. If the periods are irregular or the monthly cycle is longer the EDD is adjusted accordingly sometimes with the help of an Ultrasound scan date. The EDD does not mean that the delivery will occur on that date but it only indicates 40completed weeks of pregnancy. It is considered normal if labour starts anytime after 37 weeks of pregnancy.

What is normal weight gain during pregnancy?

The total weight gain in a healthy pregnant woman from the start of pregnancy to delivery is usually around 11-12.5 kg. As the pre-pregnant weight increases the recommended weight gain is reduced, hence obese women should ideally gain only about 7 -8 kg. Only one fourth of this is increased storage fat in the mother. The average weight gain during early pregnancy up to the 5th month is around 0.3kg/week and 0.45kg/week thereafter until delivery. Excess weight gain is associated with larger babies and difficult deliveries. So any weight gain which is in excess of the recommended weight gain for you needs to be evaluated by your doctor.

What is the importance of blood group during pregnancy?

Blood group and Rh type are routinely checked for all pregnant women. It is the Rh type, usually denoted as + (positive) or – (negative) which is of greater significance. When the mother's blood Rh type is negative and the father's type is positive there is a possibility that the baby inside is either positive or negative. In the event that the mother is negative and baby is positive there may occur a condition known as Rh incompatibility, which in severe cases might even cause death of the baby. It is uncommon in the first pregnancy but can be avoided even in subsequent pregnancies by giving the mother an injection of Anti-D within 72 hours of the delivery. This type of incompatibility does not occur if the mother has a positive Rh type. In rare cases incompatibility of the A, B, O groups is also seen.

How do I know that my baby is doing fine? How do I keep track of movements of the baby?

Around the 5th month of pregnancy you will start feeling the baby's movements, first mildly and then stronger movements by the 7th month. As long as you keep feeling the movements on and off during the day you can be reasonably sure the baby is doing fine. Towards the 8th and 9th months, the perception of these movements becomes better and can actually be counted. There are many ways to count but one simple way is to count for one hour after every meal (3 hours in a day) and if the total adds up to 10 it is fine. Another method is to count for one hour after a meal and check if there are at least 3 movements in that hour. In general, even if you do not have a count if you 'feel' that the baby has been moving less than usual it should be reported to the doctor. The doctor will confirm the well being of the baby using NST (non-stress test), USG (ultrasound scan)or a biophysical profile.

What is painless labour?

Labour is a very painful process for most women. And with recent advances in medicine, most well-equipped hospitals offer painless labour. It refers to the administration during labour of epidural analgesia. It involves injection of an analgesic drug into the spine between the layers around the nerves. This allows only the pain nerves to be numbed and one can otherwise move around but will not feel the contractions of the uterus. But the thing to remember is that labour may be prolonged when epidural analgesia is used. There are other medications that can be given in labour to reduce pain but may not as effective as the epidural injection. So discuss the advantages and risks of the type of labour analgesia offered in the hospital you are attending.

COMMON PROBLEMS DURING PREGNANCY

Nausea and vomiting: It is common in the first part of pregnancy usually until 14 weeks. It can be relieved using some medications which are safe in pregnancy. If it persists into the fifth month, other conditions like thyroid and liver disorders must be ruled out.

Constipation: Common in pregnancy due to the effect of hormones and also pressure by the baby's head on the lower intestine. Excessive straining and hard stools may lead to small fissure at the anus and mild bleeding. It can be avoided by careful attention to diet, intake of high fibre food like vegetables and fruits, plenty of water and sufficient exercise. Sometimes the doctor might prescribe a mild laxative or stool softener.

Frequent urination: Frequent urination is a common problem in the early part of pregnancy and also towards the last part of pregnancy. Nothing to worry about unless it is associated with burning or pain while passing urine.

Backache: Nearly half of all pregnant women complain of back ache. It can be relieved to a certain extent by the following measures

- Avoid excessive strain or fatigue and excessive bending, lifting weights or excessive walking.
- Try to squat instead of bending to reach down.
- Provide support to the lower back with a pillow while sitting.
- Avoid high heeled shoes.
- Place a small pillow or cushion between your thighs while sleeping.
- In the later part of pregnancy while sleeping, try placing a thin cushion below the abdomen to prevent it from falling to one side with all the weight of the pregnant uterus.

If backache is not relieved by the above measures, you must consult a doctor to check for any spine problems.

Heartburn: This is common in the latter half of pregnancy due to the pressure of the uterus upwards onto the stomach. It is usually mild and relieved with simple measures like taking small and frequent meals instead of large meals, by avoiding bending over or lying flat especially soon after a meal. Try to sit upright for 30 minutes to 1 hour after a meal. If the pain or burning is severe consult your doctor for a prescription of an antacid. Women who have been previously diagnosed with ulcers of the stomach and intestine must see a doctor for proper treatment.

Fatigue: In early pregnancy most women complain of sleepiness and a feeling of fatigue. It is merely due to the effect of a change in hormones and will soon pass by the 4th month.

Headache: Mild headaches are complained of by some women in early pregnancy and are usually due to nasal stuffiness or eye strain. They will usually disappear and may benefit from mild painkillers or local balm application and sufficient rest. Headache in the latter half of pregnancy must be reported to your doctor and the blood pressure must be checked for. If headache is persistent and troublesome you should get checked for refractory errors or in common language "short sight" or "long sight", and for other causes of headache.

Swelling of the feet: More than one third of pregnant women experience swelling of the feet due to water retention, especially during the latter half of pregnancy. It is typically less in the mornings and worse towards evening. It is relieved by lying down or keeping the feet up. It is not worrisome as long as you have checked you blood pressure and it is normal. Swelling of the feet may be the first sign of high blood pressure during pregnancy. Sometimes the swelling may be due to enlarged calf veins also called "varicose veins" and this condition might require some attention from the doctor. So always report it to the doctor so that they may ensure that the swelling is normal.

White discharge: Small amounts of non-irritating translucent mucus-like discharge is common in early pregnancy. This is mostly due to the influence of hormones released in pregnancy. But if the discharge is foamy or curdy white or yellowish, and associated with a bad smell or itching over your private parts you must report to your doctor and get appropriate treatment as this might be due to vaginal infections some of which might be sexually transmitted. Candidal or yeast infections are quite common in pregnancy especially in women with diabetes and are treatable.

Hair fall: Hair fall is not very common in pregnancy but is typically seen after delivery. This is because the roots of the hair are maintained in the growth phase throughout pregnancy due to the hormonal influence. But after delivery, when the influence is removed, there occurs a gradual hairfall which some women find worrisome. It is a normal process and the fallen hair will grow back in a few months time with good care.

Skin problems: The most common skin problems faced by pregnant women are **stretch marks** over the abdomen and breasts. The marks are usually reddish or dark coloured during pregnancy and become light after delivery. There is very little you can do to avoid them but massage with olive oil or some creams can be tried for some benefit. They only serve to lighten the marks but cannot remove them completely. You may see a skin specialist after the delivery.

Nearly 90% of women experience some **darkening of the skin** on the face, neck, thighs, near the navel etc. It is again due to the hormonal influence and will reduce significantly after delivery. Women predisposed to this pigmentation or darkening must use sunscreen when going outdoors.

Itching and rash over the skin of the abdomen and limbs is common in pregnancy. There are various causes of this and some may be associated with liver disorders and a mild form of jaundice. Some are harmless and may be relieved by anti-allergic medications and local creams and emollients. But in order to know which is harmless and which kind of rash needs to be investigated, you must consult your doctor who might even ask for an opinion from a skin specialist. In any case avoid extensive scratching which may lead to raw areas which might also get infected.

It is important to meet your doctor if you have any rash or boils near the private parts and get appropriate treatment for the infection. Some such infections can spread to the baby, especially during delivery and cause serious problems.

Bleeding from the vagina: It is rarely harmless and any amount of bleeding during pregnancy must be reported and evaluated by your doctor.

PERSONAL HABITS DURING PREGNANCY

Clothing: Wear clothes that are most comfortable to you and not too tight. Avoid fabrics that may cause too much sweating especially for Indian weather conditions. Wear inner clothes that provide sufficient support to the breasts during pregnancy as well as during breast-feeding. Tight leg wear should be avoided.

Bathing: There is no objection to bathing in a tub or otherwise during pregnancy provided the water is not very hot. There is always a risk of slipping and fall in the bathtub in the last months of pregnancy as the weight of the uterus may upset the balance.

Food Habits: As advised before, the diet should be a balanced one with sufficient protein and carbohydrates. Avoid fatty meals and too much junk food. Include at least 2 glasses of milk and generous portions of fruits and vegetables. Non-vegetarians may include meat or poultry at least twice a week taking care that it is well cooked. Avoid eating out at unhygienic places and wash all fruits and vegetables well before eating. Change in preferences or tastes is common in pregnancy and there is no need to restrict or curb yourself. Eat whatever you feel like eating as long as it is healthy. Always discuss your diet with your doctor.

Breast care: Breasts usually increase in size and weight during pregnancy and the area around the nipple might get darker. If your nipples are not prominent and somewhat depressed you might have a problem with feeding.

Hence ask your doctor to examine and teach you to evert the nipples or bring them out by massage and suction towards the latter half of pregnancy so that by the time of delivery you are able to breast feed. One must always keep the nipples and the surrounding area well moisturised and supple. Plenty of creams are available in the stores and can be applied after your doctor's advice from the 8th month onwards. Always wear well supporting inner wear to prevent sagging and discomfort.

Intercourse: In healthy pregnant women, sexual intercourse is not harmful until the end of 8th month. But in women with risk of abortion and preterm labour it should be avoided. It is better to discuss with your doctor; especially if it is your first pregnancy. In any case it is always better if a condom is used in order to prevent any sexually transmitted infections.

The changes that occur during and after pregnancy are normal fundamental changes in every woman's life but they have a profound effect on the sexuality and sexual life of the couple. It is different for different couples and varies from woman to woman.

There is a physical aspect and a psychological aspect to this. There are certain changes in the body like abdominal distension, heaviness in the lower abdomen and pelvis, decreased vaginal secretion leading to reduced lubrication, infections of the genital area etc which make intercourse a not so pleasurable experience. But there are women who do not get affected by these changes and actually enjoy intercourse much more during pregnancy.

The desire for intercourse may vary in women and is affected by some of the following factors:

- Whether it was a planned pregnancy.
- Whether any treatment for intertility was taken or not.
- The general health of the woman and associated medical conditions
- The fears associated with pregnancy like fear of harming the baby
- Stress at home or workplace
- Relationship with the partner

Sexual intercourse is normally safe in pregnancy provided both partners are interested and they do not have any discomfort. Penetrative sex may be uncomfortable for some and such couples may try alternative positions and non-penetrative stimulation. A non-irritant lubricant may be used to help lack of natural lubrication. In most cases the doctors do not advise abstinence but there are some conditions where intercourse is best avoided like:

- A history of recurrent miscarriages
- Vaginal Bleeding or spotting
- Low lying placenta
- Leaking amniotic fluid
- Preterm labor in the previous pregnancies

In India many doctors routinely advise avoidance of intercourse in the first 3-4 months as this is the most delicate period and most of the miscarriages occur within this time. In addition to this, one must pay attention to hygiene during intercourse as infections acquired by the woman during this time might affect the pregnancy.

After delivery

Sexual health and attitudes after delivery are greatly affected by many physical, psychological ,social and interpersonal relationships. Sexual activity and satisfaction is reduced for nearly 1 year after delivery. This may be due to:

- Pain around the vagina, more so in women who have had stitches after a normal vaginal delivery. Until the stitches heal well the pain may persist and this is the reason intercourse is best avoided for one month after a vaginal delivery.
- Women who have had cesarean section may be advised abstinence for 2-3 months due to the abdominal stitches which take around 3 months for all the layers to heal.
- Initially the woman may experience lack of lubrication due to reduced vaginal secretions and a simple lubricant like K-Y Jelly may help.
- If the intercourse is painful and distressing always consult the doctor.
- Proper family planning advice is essential to ensure there is no stress or fear of an unwanted pregnancy. One must remember that a pregnancy can occur even if periods do not resume after delivery.

Smoking: Smoking causes damage to the baby inside, preterm labour and low birth weight babies. Even stillbirths have been reported in women who smoked during pregnancy. Hence it is to be avoided in all women who are planning for or are already pregnant.

Alcohol: Alcohol in pregnancy is extremely dangerous to the baby and must be avoided even before the pregnancy is diagnosed i.e. when the couple starts planning for a pregnancy.

Caffeine: Caffeine is not generally harmful in pregnancy when taken in small amounts, but has been found to cause abortions if more than 4-5 cups of coffee are taken per day.

Illicit drugs: Drugs like opium, heroin, sleeping pills etc are to be avoided during pregnancy and breast feeding.

Sleep: Sleep is usually excessive in the early months due to hormonal influence, but usually becomes normal after the 4th month. In the last 2 months sleep might be difficult due to the discomfort caused by the heavy pregnant uterus and associated back ache. You must try sleeping to one side most often and not on the back as this allows better blood supply to the uterus. Try the suggested precautions for preventing backache and do not take any sleeping pills. In women who have pregnancy complications it is suggested that they take a few hours rest in the day and sufficient (6-8 hours) rest at night.

Post delivery period

All is not over with the baby out of the uterus. Now that the baby has finally arrived safely be prepared for the joys and responsibilities of motherhood.

Breast feeding has been discussed extensively in the sections on care of babies; hence in this section we will discuss more about the care of the mother. After delivery the woman is exhausted and needs rest. You should take rest while the baby sleeps and remember to make the baby suckle at the breast every 2 hours.

- You might experience pain either due to the stitches put after a vaginal delivery or after a caesarean section. Ask your doctor for sufficient pain relief.
- After a normal delivery keep yourself and the stitches clean by bathing and by washing the private parts with warm water after every visit to pass urine or stools.
- After a caesarean most hospitals advise sponging the body with warm water in order to keep clean. You may have a bath from the 3rd or 4th day with assistance.
- Breast hygiene is extremely important and remember to wipe with warm water before and 'after' feeding the baby. Cracked nipples may be a problem and must be treated with massage of prescribed ointment and hygiene.
- You will have bleeding in moderate amounts the first 2-3 days and the

discharge will become more yellowish or white as days go by. If the bleeding is heavy and you feel faint you must report to the doctor. Some women experience irregular bleeding in small amounts upto one month of delivery usually a caesarean section.

- If the vaginal discharge is yellowish and foul –smelling or associated with fever you must report to the doctor.
- Always use clean sanitary pads and not pieces of cloth for soaking the bleeding or discharge.
- After a caesarean delivery avoid straining and bending over until 3 months as the internal stitches take time to heal and straining may cause imperfect healing.
- After a normal delivery avoid straining for atleast 2 months to prevent weakening of the supports to the uterus. Ask your doctor for advice regarding post-delivery exercises.
- You may resume your routine exercise schedule by the 4th month after delivery.
- Discuss options for spacing of the next pregnancy with your doctor and spouse and start birth control by the end of 2nd month.
- Sexual intercourse may be resumed after the second month and after birth control measures have been taken.
- Remember to keep your appointment with your doctor after 6 weeks of delivery.

❑❑❑

41

Related Laws

M.V. Durga Prasad
(BA, LLB)

I have given birth to 3 female children in expectation of a son. I am pregnant now. I do not want to go ahead with my pregnancy unless I am sure about giving birth to a son this time.

Law prohibits sex selection and conducting any tests for the said purpose. It is an offence under law.

Law prohibits prenatal diagnostic procedures, except with the written consent of the pregnant woman and for the limited purposes of detection of the following abnormalities, namely:

Chromosomal abnormalities

Genetic metabolic diseasesHaemoglobinopathies

Sex-linked genetic diseasesCongenital anomalies

Any other abnormalities or disease specified by the Central Supervisory Board

No written consent of the pregnant woman shall be given unless she was explained about all known side effects and after effects of such procedures in the language she understands and the written consent is taken in the form prescribed. Such pre- natal diagnostic procedures will be conducted only by qualified persons in registered Genetic Counseling Centres or Genetic Laboratory or Genetic Clinic which is registered in accordance with law.

The qualified person must ensure and record in writing that anyone of the following conditions is fulfilled before conducting such tests:

- Age of the pregnant woman is above 35 years of age
- The pregnant woman has undergone two or more spontaneous abortions or fetal loss.

- The pregnant had been exposed to potentially teratogenic agents such as drugs, radiation, infection or chemicals.
- The pregnant woman or her spouse has a family history of mental retardation or physical deformities such as spasticity, or any other genetic disease.
- Any other condition as may be specified by the board.
- Even the husband or relative of the pregnant woman is prohibited from seeking or encouraging such tests, except for the aforesaid purposes. In case of ultrasonography, the clinic must keep complete record thereof.

I want to go for abortion. Tell me more about the legal aspects.

Pregnancies may be terminated only by:

a) a registered medical practitioner,

b) in the hospital established and maintained by the government or approved by the government

c) in case of pregnancy of 12 weeks or less at least a medical practitioner or in case of pregnancy exceeding 12 weeks but not 20 weeks, at least 2 medical practitioners in good faith give opinion that the continuance of pregnancy would involve a risk to the life of the pregnant woman or of grave injury to her physical or mental health or there is substantial risk to the child if born.

However, law gives leverage in case of pregnancy by rape. Similarly, the married parents are also given the liberty of abortion in case of failure of any device or method used for the purpose of limiting the number of children fails. In case of the minor girl less than 18 years of age or major girl who is not mentally sound, the consent of the guardian shall be taken; and in case of others, the consent of the pregnant woman alone shall be taken.

I do not have children. I want to adopt a child. Tell me about the legal aspects.

Adoption is not a secular law. Only Hindus are entitled to adopt a child under their personal law. Under the condition of Hindu law, any Hindu can adopt only one son and one daughter. If they already have a son, daughter, grandson or granddaughter through a son, they cannot adopt any other son or daughter. In case of a married Hindu, the consent of the spouse is necessary. Apart from the natural parents, even a guardian who is appointed by the Will of the child's parents or a guardian appointed by the court may also give consent for adoption.

In case of a child, whose parentage is not known or is abandoned or both the parents are known to have been dead and finally renounced the world, the previous permission of the Court as well as the consent of the Guardian must be taken.

A widow or unmarried girl can also adopt a child, provided that the other conditions are also satisfied. In case of Hindus who are not married, there must be a custom in the community permitting such adoption. When a widower or bachelor adopts a child, the wife who marries him subsequently becomes a step-mother, but not a mother.

For adopting a child one should be of sound mind and attained the age of discretion. There shall be age difference between the adoptive father and daughter and adoptive mother and son by 21 years. For adoption, the consent of the natural father is a must.

No child who is already adopted can be readopted by others. No child 15 years or more shall be adopted, unless there is a custom or usage in the community of the parties to adoption. All the parties must be Hindus, including the child.

The law does not prescribe any legal formalities for a valid adoption. The giving and taking of the child by the natural and adoptive parents respectively must be expressed and evident. No agreement or deed is required for a valid adoption. The adoption can also be proved by oral evidence. But, such a course may be difficult and may even become controversial. Therefore, it is better to have an adoption deed drafted, signed by both the natural and adoptive parents and registered. Once it is registered, there is a presumption under the law that it is valid.

No money shall be paid or received in consideration of adoption or any reward for adoption.

Consequences of a valid adoption are:

By adoption the child is just like a natural born child and gets transplanted to the adoptive family and he shall be deemed to be the child of the adoptive parents, for all legal purposes, with effect from the date of adoption and his relationship also shall be deemed to have been severed from the natural parents, except for the purpose of marriage. That means he cannot marry a person, whom he could not have married (on account of prohibitory relationship), before such adoption.

He does not lose rights already vested in him before adoption. Whatever properties she or he has already inherited will not be lost.

The adoption will not affect the properties already vested in any third person.

Unless they have agreed otherwise, the adoptive parents are entitled to dispose off their properties by way of Will or any other document as they like and the adoption does not affect such rights.

I am not a Hindu. Can I adopt?

As already said, adoption is not a secular law and it applies only to Hindus. A person can apply for being appointed as Guardian under the Guardian and Wards Act, 1980 to the district court. Without such permission from the Court, if any one takes custody of the child, he or she may be running the risk or action from the natural parents or person claiming to be the guardian. Taking a child without the consent of the natural parent or guardian amounts to an offence of kidnapping. Further, no legal right can be exercised over the child unless one is appointed as guardian by the Court.

Is there any restriction on sale or use of infant foods?

Yes. Law regulates production, supply and distribution of infant milk substitutes, feedingbottles and infant foods with a view to the protection and promotion of breast-feeding and ensuring the proper use of infant foods. Any food (whatever name called) being marketed or otherwise represented as a complement to mother's milk, to meet the growing nutritional needs of the infant after the age of four months is called infant food. If it substitutes partially or totally mother's milk, it is called infant milk substitute. Law prohibits advertisements and promotion of infant milk substitutes, feeding bottles and infant foods. No one shall contact any pregnant woman or mother of an infant for purpose of promoting the use or sale of infant milk substitutes or feeding bottles. No one can even gift them except to orphanage or offer any such inducement for their use or sale. Any material which seeks to educate the pregnant woman or mother of an infant shall include information relating to benefits and superiority of breast feeding, preparation and continuation of breast feeding and harmful effects on breast feeding due to partial adoption of bottle feeding and health hazards of improper use of infant milk substitutes and feeding bottles and all other related information.

I want to buy infant foods. What precautions should I take?

Every milk substitute or infant food shall have a label indicating in conspicuous manner, an, "IMPORTANT NOTICE" in English or Hindi and a statement, "MOTHER'S MILK IS BEST FOR YOUR BABY". It shall indicate all the precautions for proper use of infant milk substitute and warn against health hazards in the manner prescribed. The protein efficiency ratio shall be a minimum of 2.5. There shall not be any statement implying "Recommended by the Medical Profession". There shall not be use of any words like "Humanised" or "Maternalised" or "Energy Food", "Full Protein Food", "Complete Food" or "Health Food" or any other similar expression in any language. It shall also contain, (i) the approximate composition of nutrients per 100 grams of product including its energy value in calories; (ii) the storage conditions specifically stating "Store in cool and dry place in an air container" or the like; (iii) the feeding chart and direction for use and instruction for discarding leftover feed, the batch number and date of manufacture; (iv) instructions for use of measuring scoop (level or heaped) and the quantity per scoop; (v) the prescribed period by which the infant milk substitutes or the infant food, as the case may be, is to be consumed; (vi) the Protein Efficiency Ration (PER) which shall be minimum of 2.5 if the product other than the infant milk substitutes and infant foods is claimed to have high quality protein.

It should conform to all the standards specified for such substitutes or food under the Prevention of Food Adulteration Act; and if no such standards are specified such food shall not be sold unless permitted by the Central Government. However, there shall be no reference to the Acts and Rules or Comments on explanations thereto in the label. In addition to the above, the container shall have relevance standard mark (ISI) of the Bureau of the Indian Standards.

Therefore you will have to ensure the above requirements before buying any infant food. Please note that noncompliance with the above requirements makes the infant food illegal and liable to be confiscated.

❑❑❑

Appendices

Birth to 24 months: Boys
Head circumference-for-age and Weight-for-length percentiles

NAME ____________________

RECORD # ____________

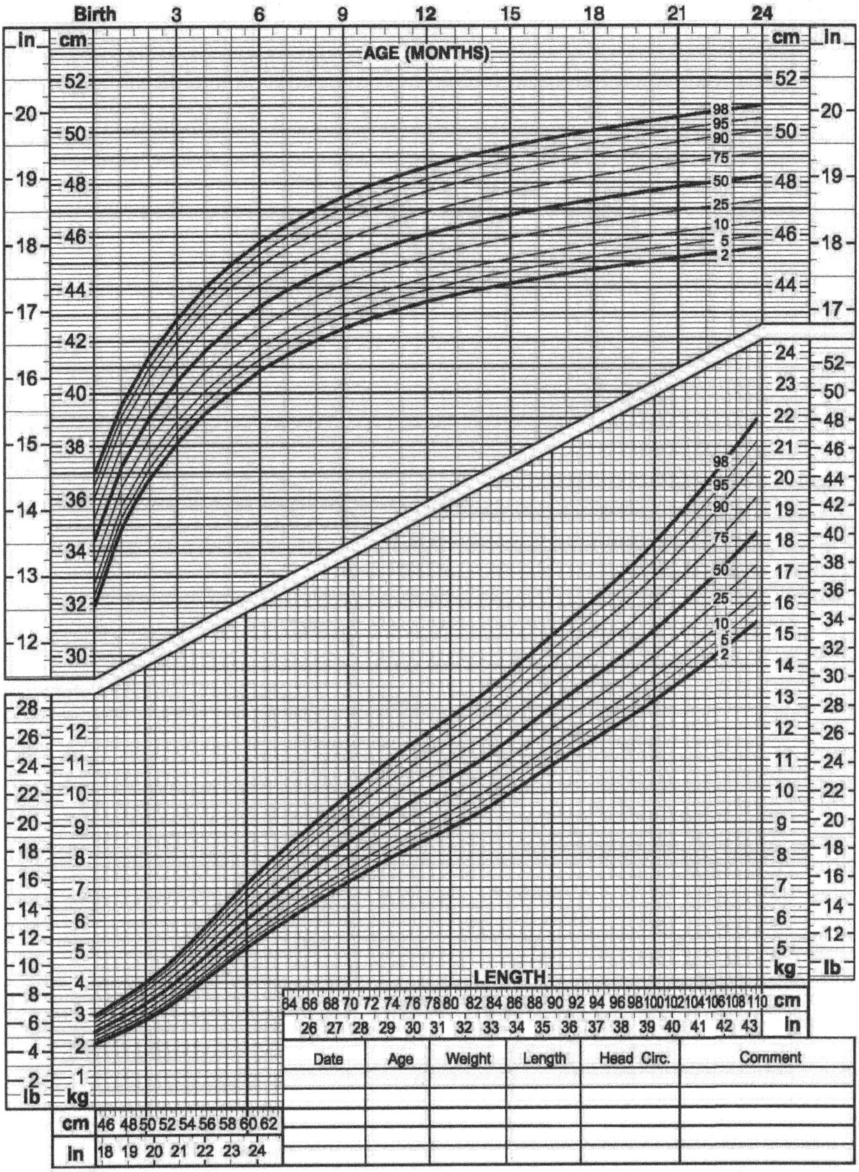

Date	Age	Weight	Length	Head Circ.	Comment

Published by the Centers for Disease Control and Prevention, November 1, 2009
SOURCE: WHO Child Growth Standards (http://www.who.int/childgrowth/en)

Birth to 24 months: Boys
Length-for-age and Weight-for-age percentiles

NAME ______________________

RECORD # ____________

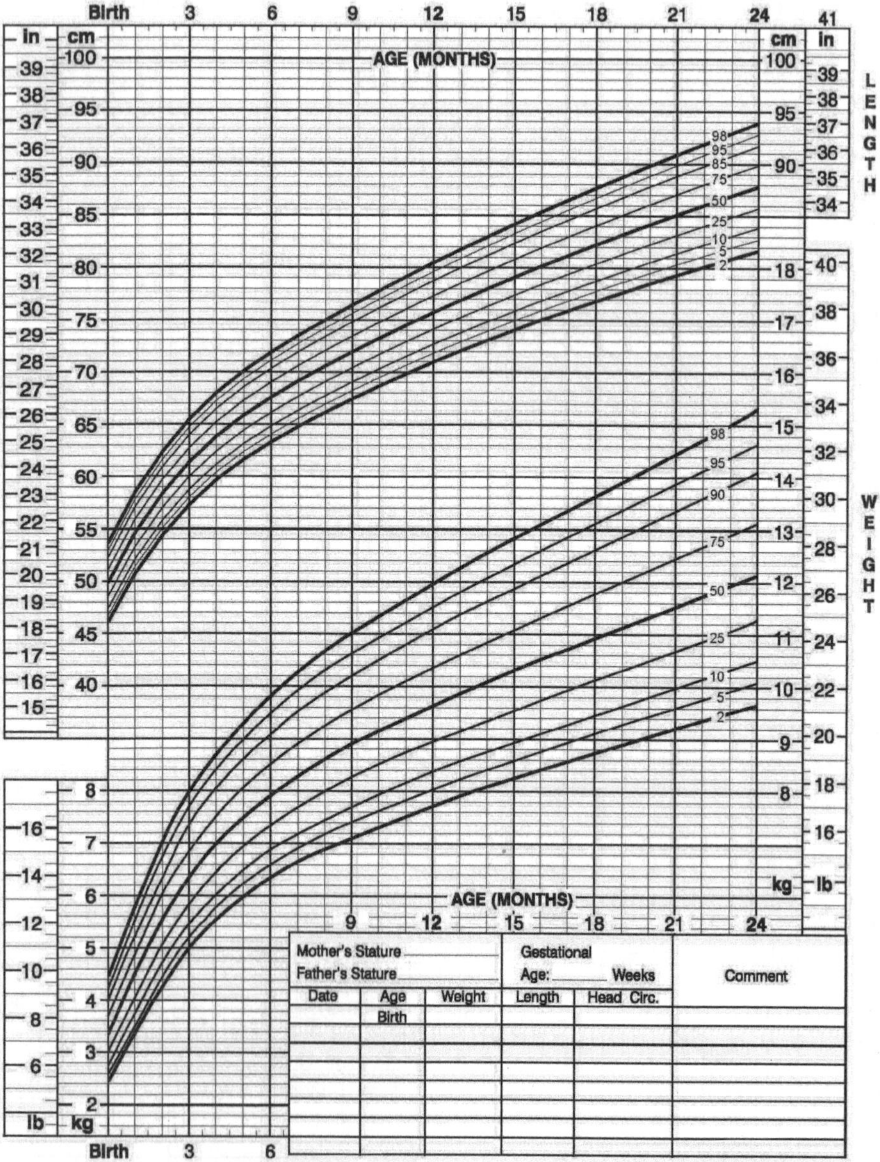

Published by the Centers for Disease Control and Prevention, November 1, 2009
SOURCE: WHO Child Growth Standards (http://www.who.int/childgrowth/en)

Birth to 24 months: Girls
Head circumference-for-age and
Weight-for-length percentiles

NAME ____________________

RECORD # ____________

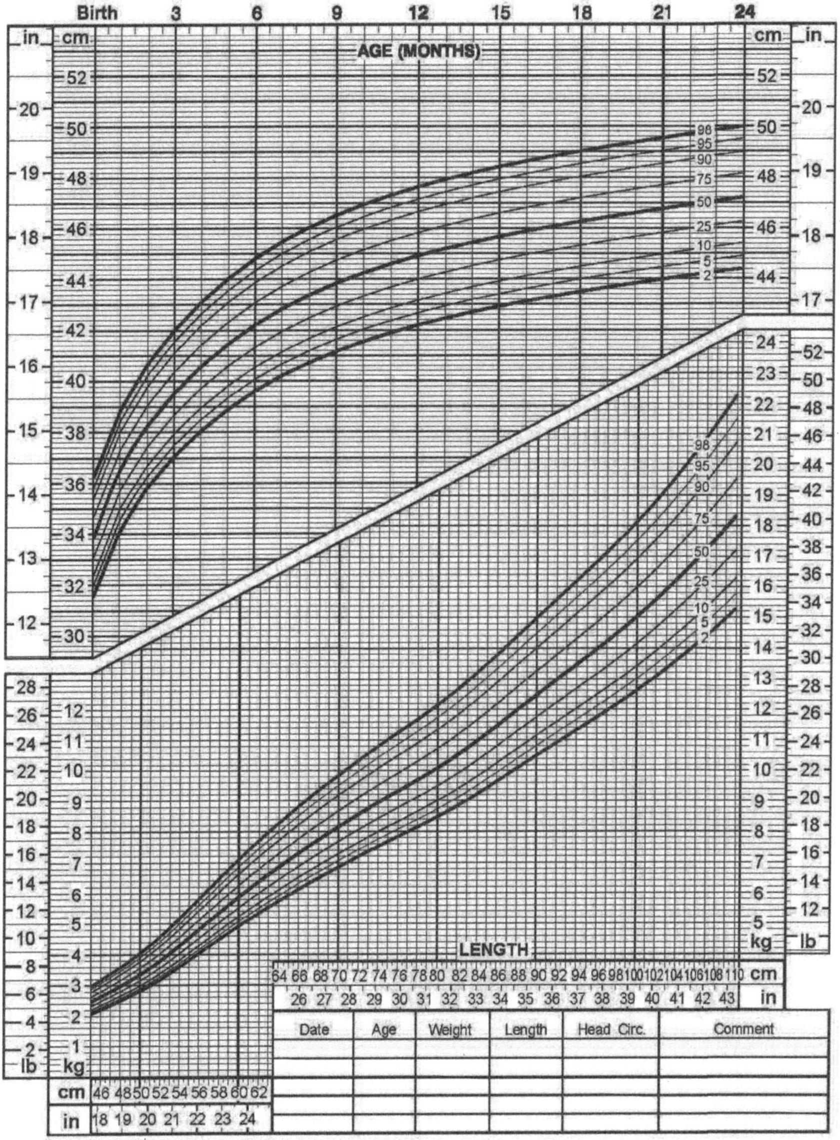

Date	Age	Weight	Length	Head Circ.	Comment

Published by the Centers for Disease Control and Prevention, November 1, 2009
SOURCE: WHO Child Growth Standards (http://www.who.int/childgrowth/en)

Birth to 24 months: Girls
Length-for-age and Weight-for-age percentiles

NAME ______________________

RECORD # ______

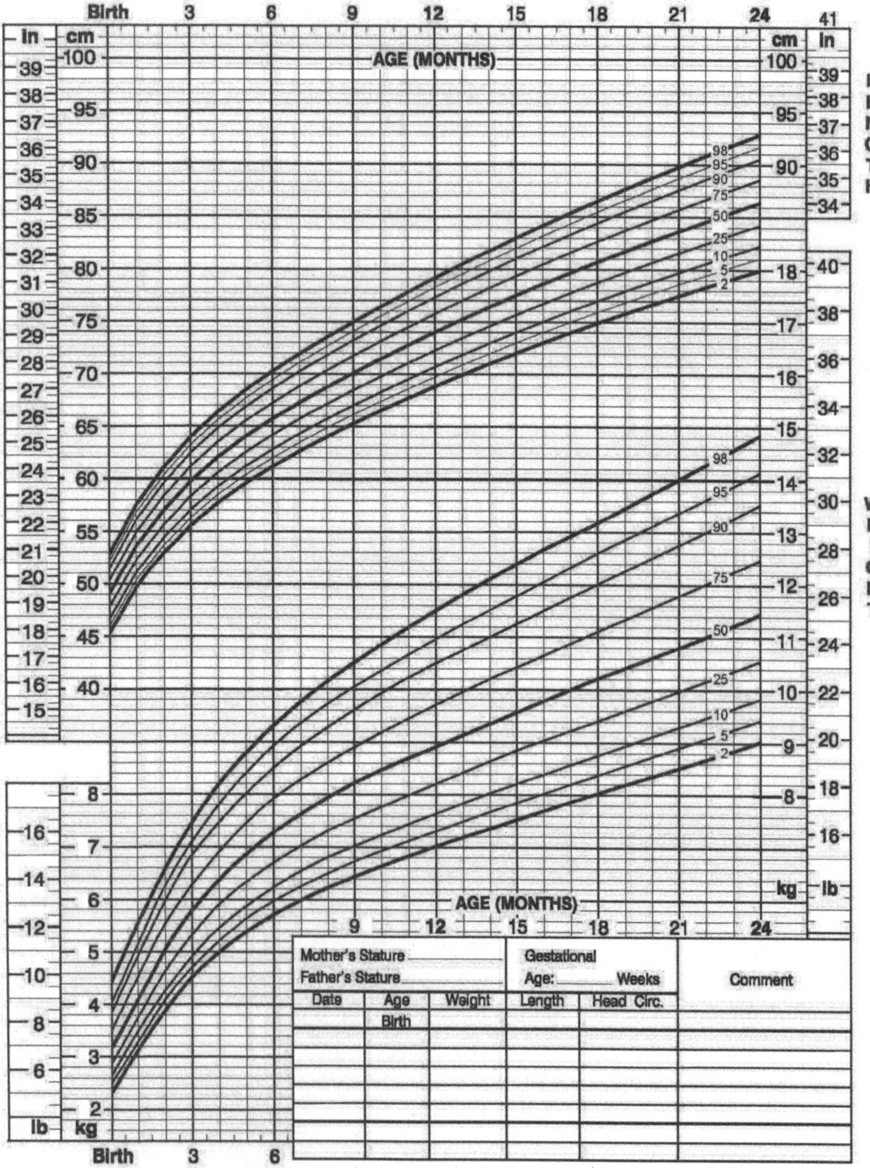

Published by the Centers for Disease Control and Prevention, November 1, 2009
SOURCE: WHO Child Growth Standards (http://www.who.int/childgrowth/en)

CDC Growth Charts: United States

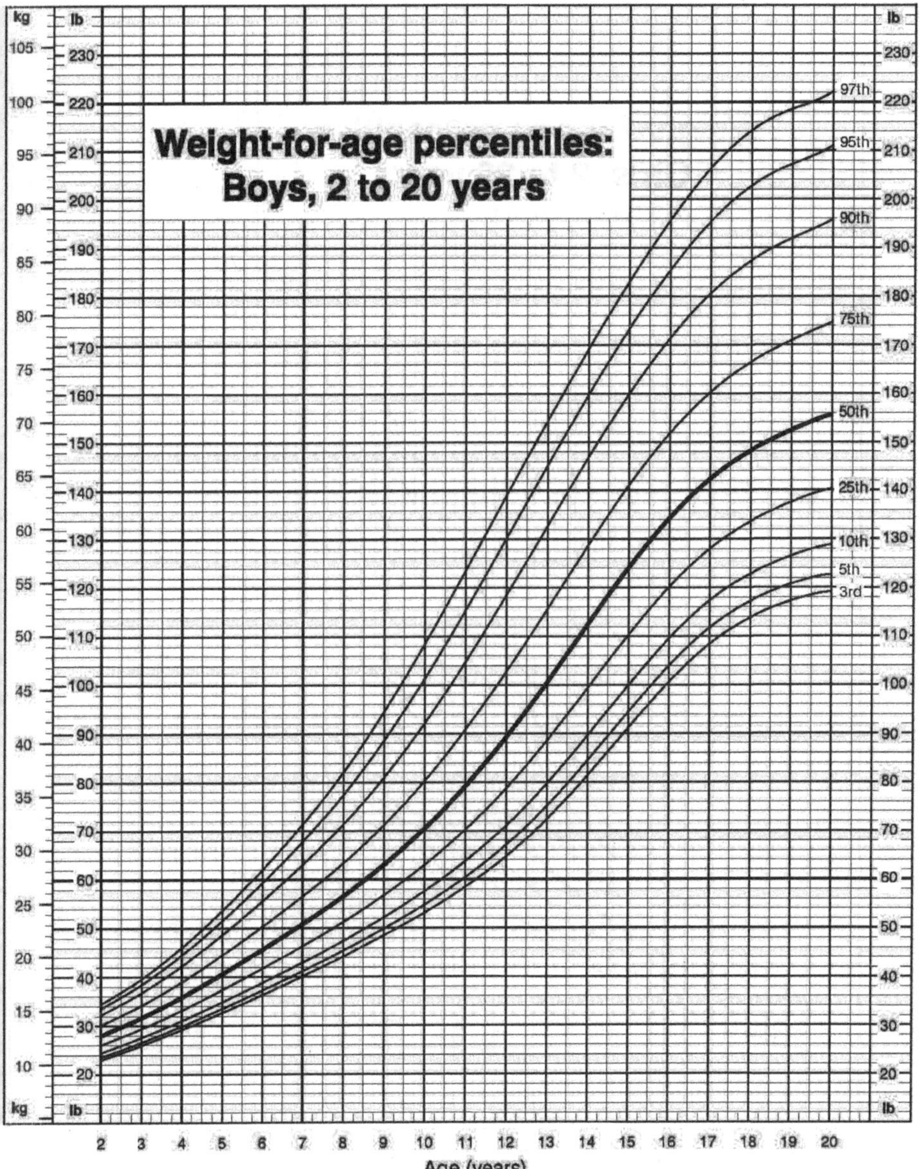

Published May 30, 2000.

SOURCE: Developed by the National Center for Health Statistics in collaboration with the National Center for Chronic Disease Prevention and Health Promotion (2000).

CDC SAFER • HEALTHIER • PEOPLE™

CDC Growth Charts: United States

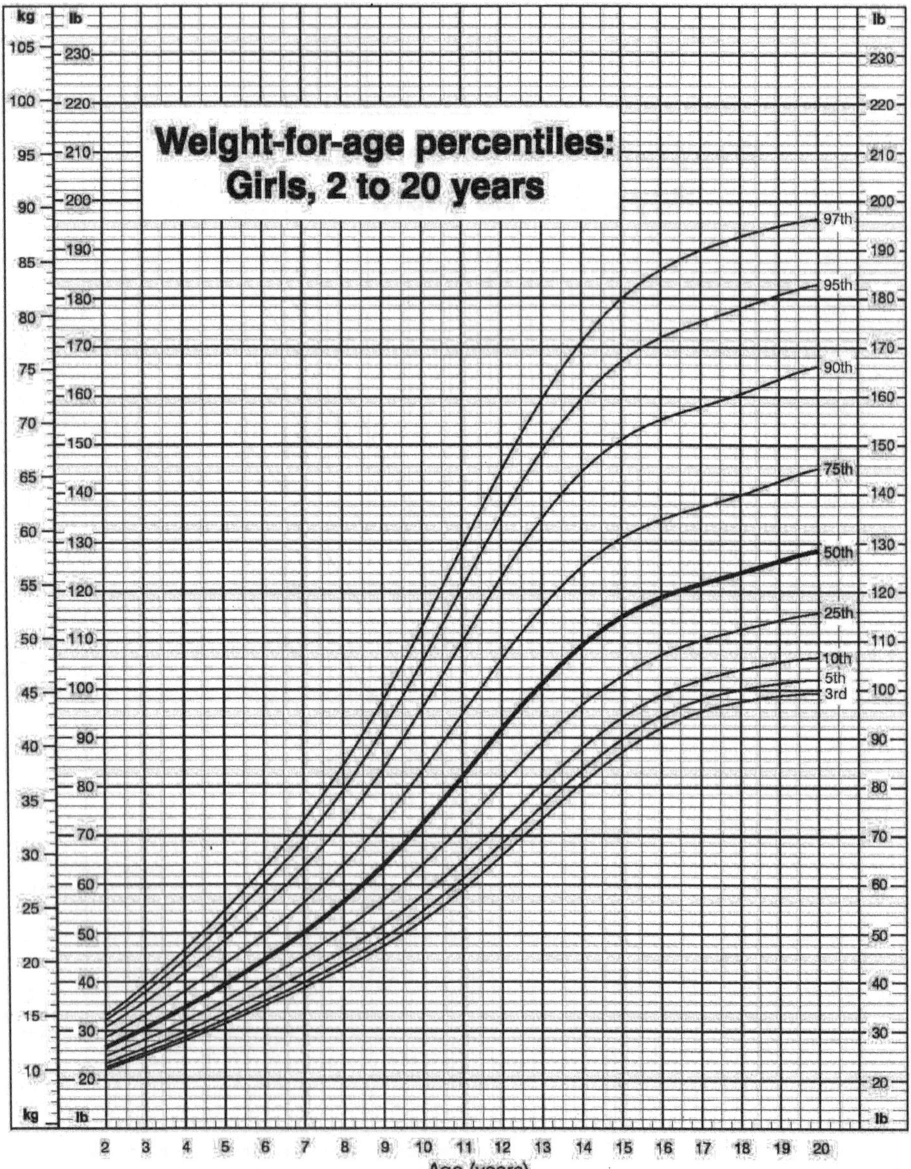

Published May 30, 2000.

SOURCE: Developed by the National Center for Health Statistics in collaboration with the National Center for Chronic Disease Prevention and Health Promotion (2000).

SAFER • HEALTHIER • PEOPLE™

CDC Growth Charts: United States

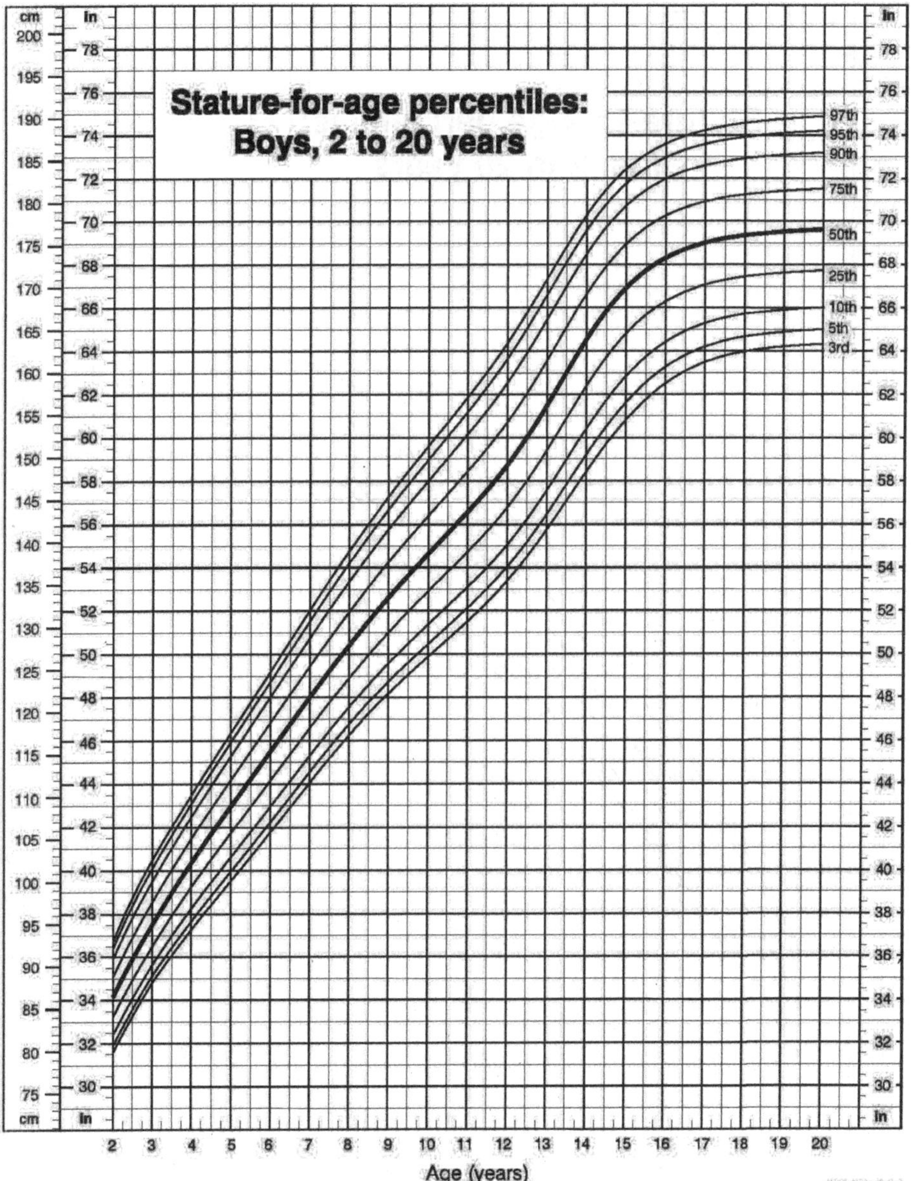

Published May 30, 2000.

SOURCE: Developed by the National Center for Health Statistics in collaboration with the National Center for Chronic Disease Prevention and Health Promotion (2000).

CDC SAFER • HEALTHIER • PEOPLE™

CDC Growth Charts: United States

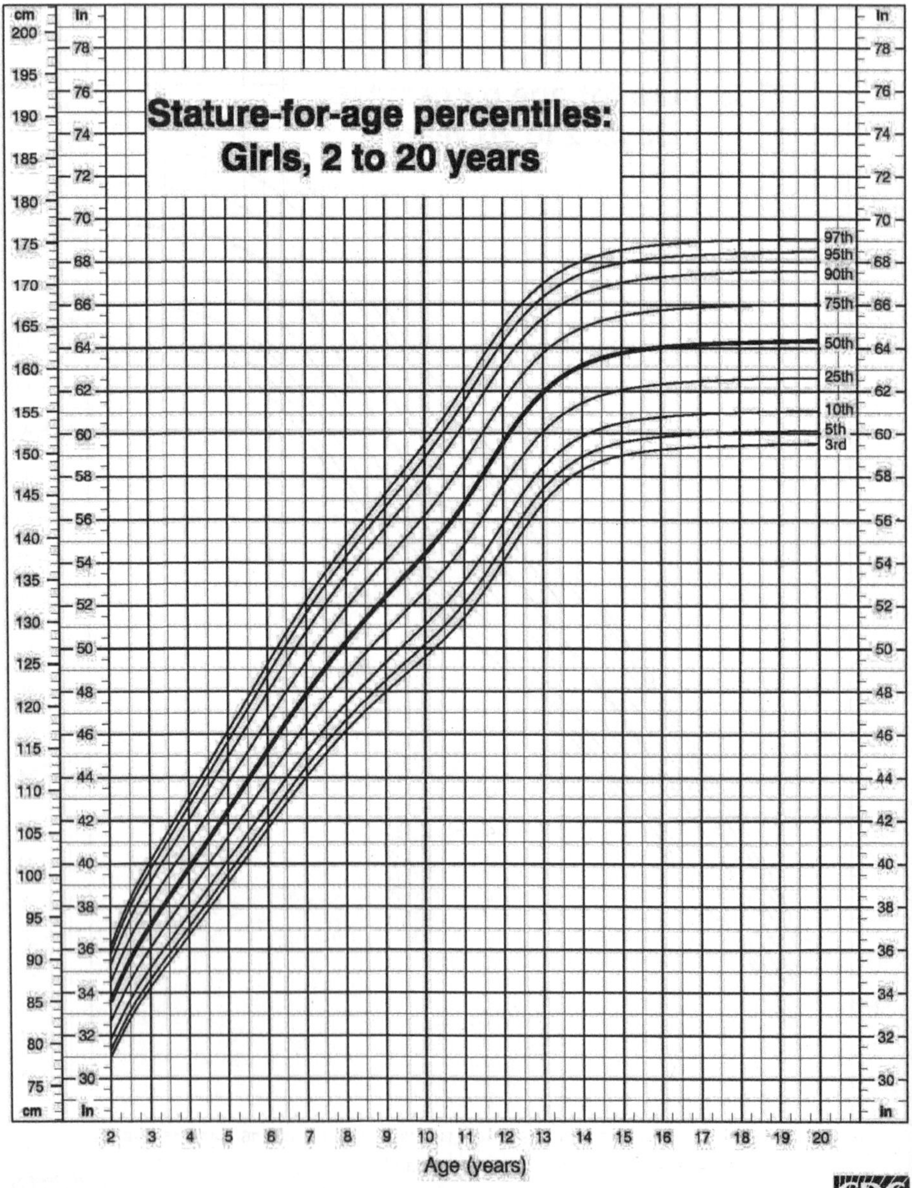

Published May 30, 2000.
SOURCE: Developed by the National Center for Health Statistics in collaboration with the National Center for Chronic Disease Prevention and Health Promotion (2000).

SAFER·HEALTHIER·PEOPLE

CDC Growth Charts: United States

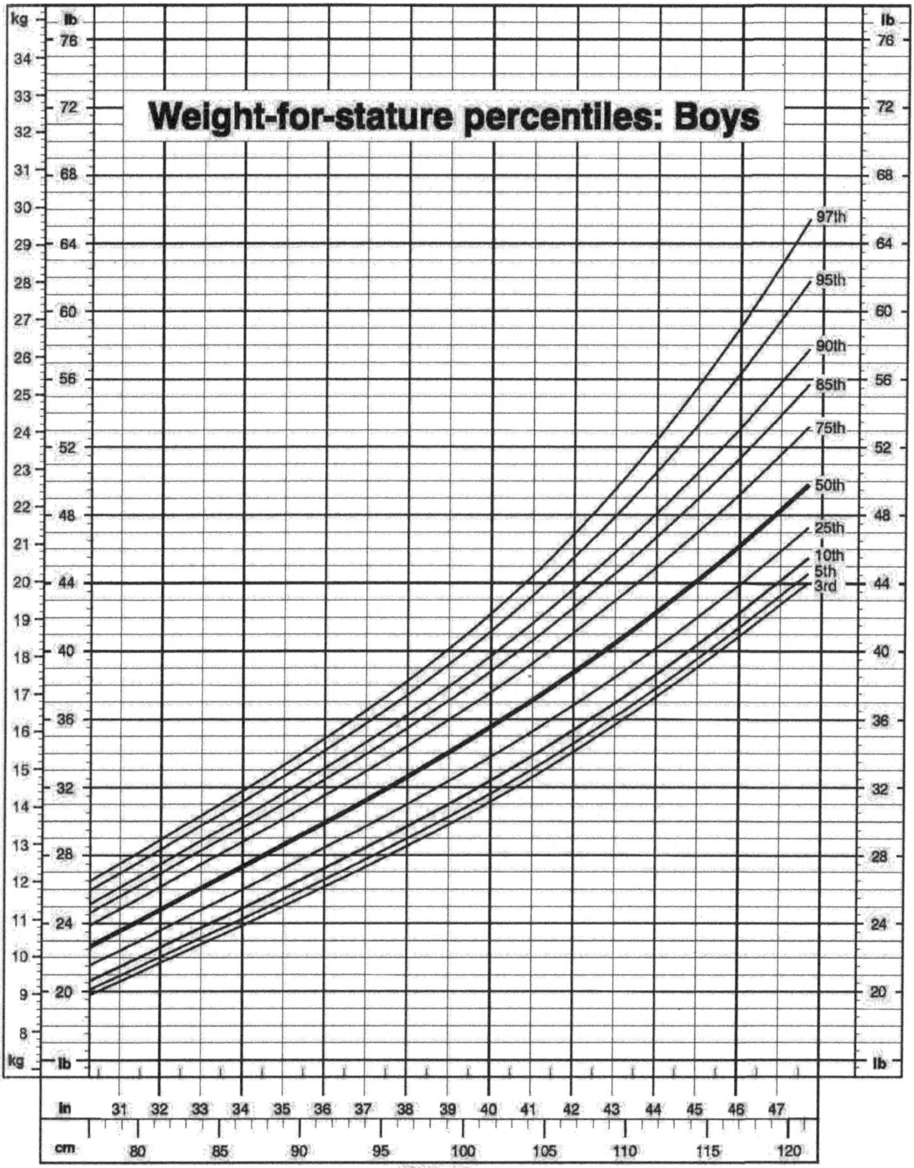

Published May 30, 2000 (modified 11/21/00).
SOURCE: Developed by the National Center for Health Statistics in collaboration with the National Center for Chronic Disease Prevention and Health Promotion (2000).

CDC SAFER·HEALTHIER·PEOPLE™

CDC Growth Charts: United States

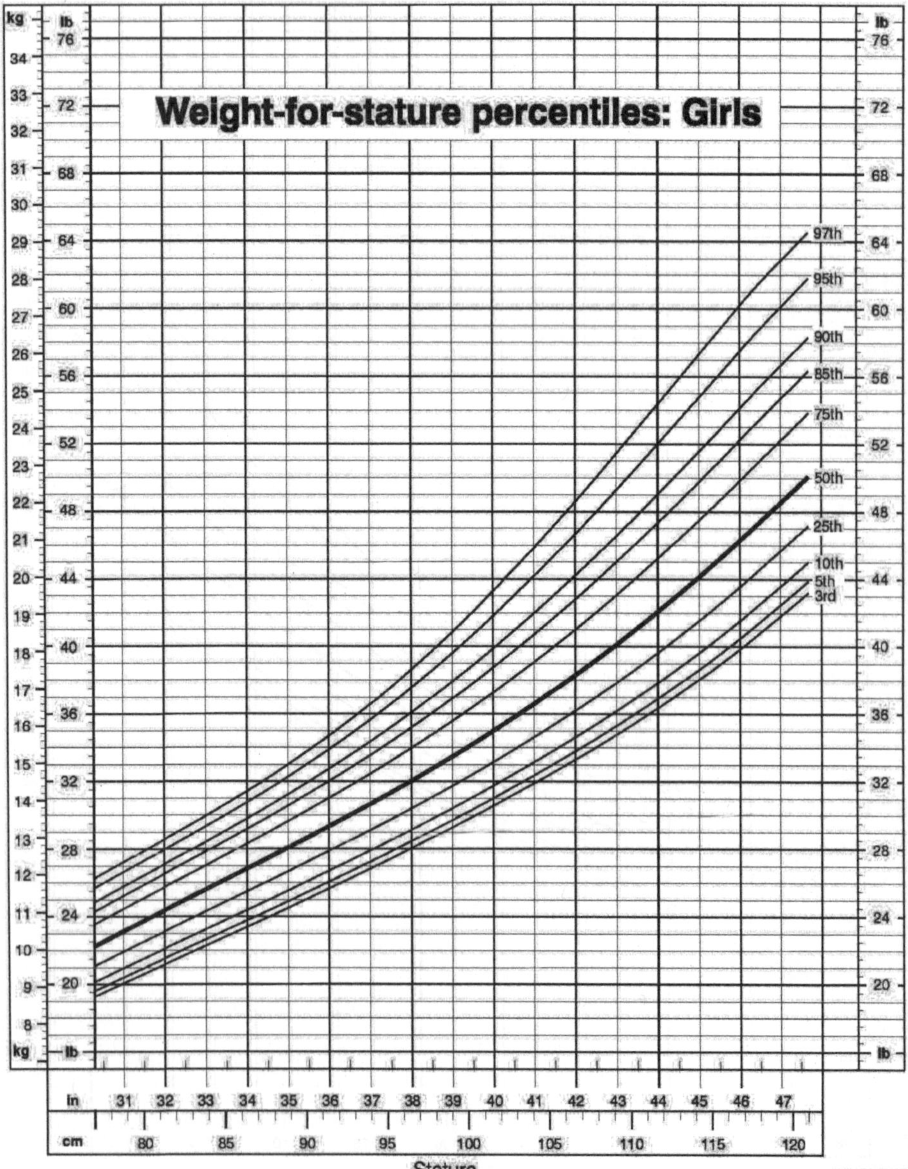

Published May 30, 2000 (modified 11/21/00).
SOURCE: Developed by the National Center for Health Statistics in collaboration with the National Center for Chronic Disease Prevention and Health Promotion (2000).

SAFER • HEALTHIER • PEOPLE™

CDC Growth Charts: United States

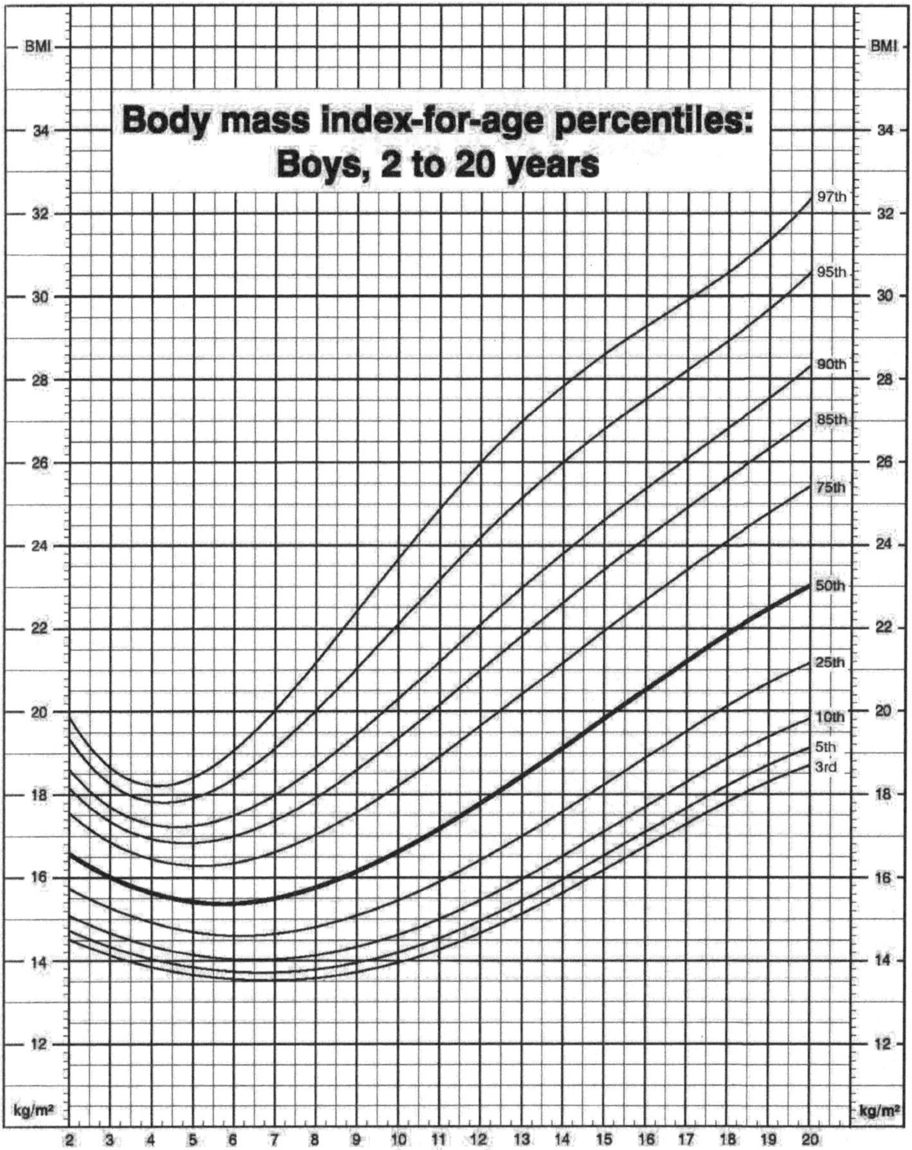

Published May 30, 2000.
SOURCE: Developed by the National Center for Health Statistics in collaboration with the National Center for Chronic Disease Prevention and Health Promotion (2000).

SAFER · HEALTHIER · PEOPLE™

CDC Growth Charts: United States

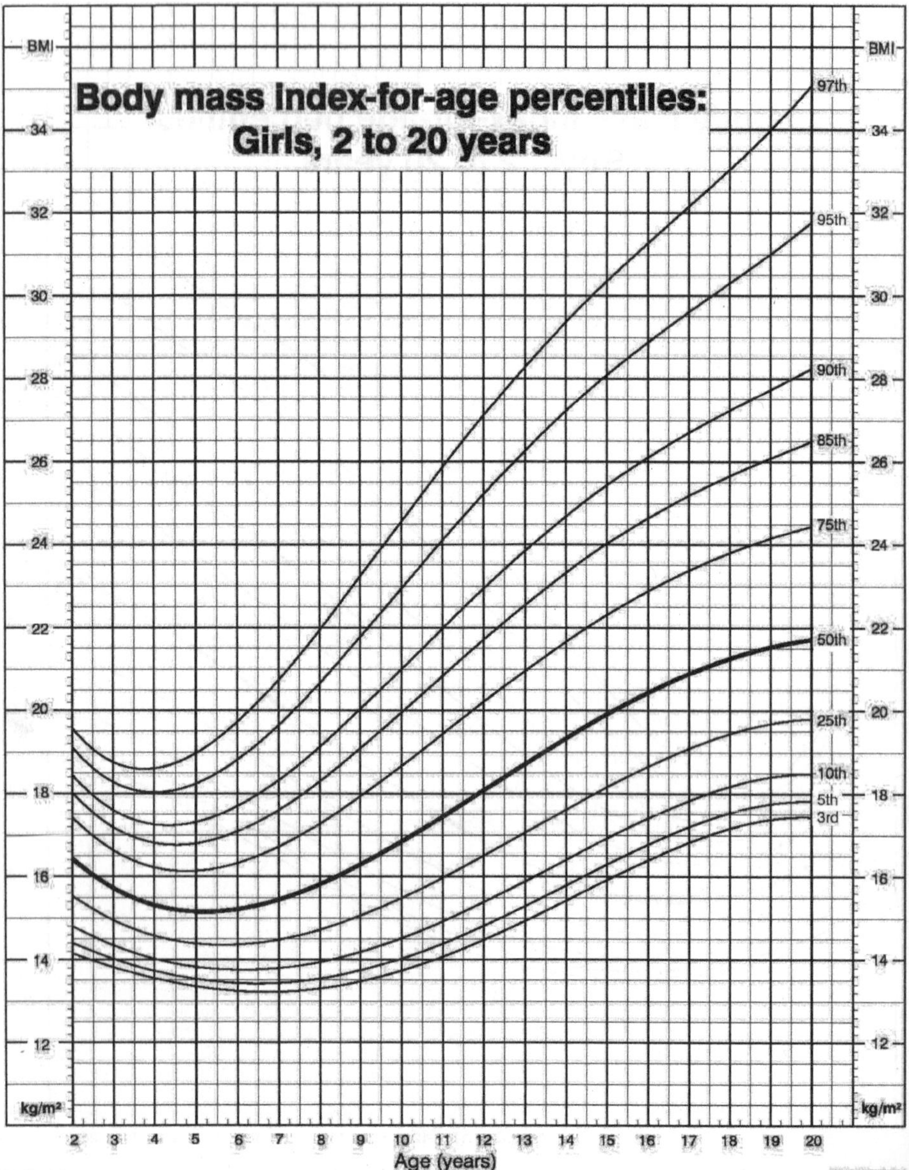

Published May 30, 2000.

SOURCE: Developed by the National Center for Health Statistics in collaboration with the National Center for Chronic Disease Prevention and Health Promotion (2000).

CDC

SAFER · HEALTHIER · PEOPLE